QUALITY
QUOTES

Also available from ASQ Quality Press

A History of Managing for Quality:
The Evolution, Trends, and Future Directions of Managing for Quality
J. M. Juran, editor-in-chief

The Quality Toolbox
Nancy Tague

The Change Agents' Handbook:
A Survival Guide for Quality Improvement Champions
David W. Hutton

Total Quality Service:
A Simplified Approach to Using the Baldrige Award Criteria
Sheila Kessler

Baldrige Award Winning Quality:
How to Interpret the Malcolm Baldrige Award Criteria, Sixth Edition
Mark Graham Brown

Rx for Business:
A Troubleshooting Guide for Building a High-Performance Organization
Mark Graham Brown, Darcy E. Hitchcock, and Marsha L. Willard

Actual Experiences of a CEO:
How to Make Continuous Improvement in Manufacturing
Succeed for Your Company
Hank McHale

Quality Progress Collection CD-ROM
ASQ

To request a complimentary catalog of publications, call 800-248-1946.

QUALITY QUOTES

Hélio Gomes

ASQ Quality Press
Milwaukee, Wisconsin

Quality Quotes
Hélio Gomes

Library of Congress Cataloging-in-Publication Data

Gomes, Hélio.
   Quality quotes / Hélio Gomes.
      p. cm.
   Includes bibliographical references and index.
   ISBN 0-87389-407-3 (alk. paper)
   1. Total quality management—Quotations. maxims, etc.   I. Title.
HD62.15.G658   1996
658.5′62—dc20   96-8141
                                             CIP

10 9 8 7 6 5

ISBN 0-87389-407-3

Acquisitions Editor: Roger Holloway
Project Editor: Jeanne W. Bohn

ASQ Mission: To facilitate continuous improvement and increase customer satisfaction by identifying, communicating, and promoting the use of quality principles, concepts, and technologies; and thereby be recognized throughout the world as the leading authority on, and champion for, quality.

Attention: Schools and Corporations
ASQ Quality Press books, audiotapes, videotapes, and software are available at quantity discounts with bulk purchases for business, educational, or instructional use. For information, please contact ASQ Quality Press at 800-248-1946, or write to ASQ Quality Press, P.O. Box 3005, Milwaukee, WI 53201-3005.

For a free copy of the ASQ Quality Press Publications Catalog, including ASQ membership information, call 800-248-1946.

Printed in the United States of America

∞ Printed on acid-free paper

American Society for Quality

Quality Press
611 East Wisconsin Avenue
Milwaukee, Wisconsin 53202
Call toll free 800-248-1946
www.asq.org
http://qualitypress.asq.org
http://standardsgroup.asq.org
http://e-standards.asq.org
E-mail: authors@asq.org

For Joseph Juran, W. Edwards Deming, Tom Peters, Kaoru Ishikawa, Robert Waterman Jr., Philip Crosby, and all the other 550-plus "sources" who have, literally, made this book possible.

Contents

Preface

Next to the originator of a good sentence is the first quoter of it.
—Ralph Waldo Emerson, *Quotations and Originality*

Quality Quotes is one of the primary results of five years of extensive reading, and intensive note-taking, during my research in the field of quality. As I read, I kept an eye out for pithy, inspirational, thought-provoking, or just plain entertaining sayings on quality. I began with books by major American and Japanese quality experts (Juran, Deming, Crosby, Ishikawa, and Imai, among others). When that coverage was complete, I expanded the quotation base to include many individuals in addition to quality professionals (poets, public figures, philosophers, entertainers, etc.) from all eras, as well as a diversity of media (newspaper and TV advertising, company slogans, magazine articles). Why didn't I just buy myself an anthology? I had earlier discovered that a book on quality quotations just didn't exist.

This book fills a substantial void in the quality field. It is a unique set of 1500-plus quotes, from 550 authors, representing 18 countries and all major historical periods, on practically every aspect of quality. The book covers quality in the broadest sense—including 36 topics, ranging from definitions to caveats in total quality management implementation.

Quality Quotes appeals to a broad audience. It is an ideal companion for businesspeople everywhere, in all industries. It is particularly useful to quality professionals (and prospective quality professionals), to those engaged in employee education and training programs, and to anyone involved in the implementation of a quality system. These professionals can draw extensively from the book, seeking the appropriate and precise quote that will enhance their presentations. They will discover that a good quote can help get their point across, add extra credibility and flavor to their point of view, or serve as inspiration in the initial preparation of a written or oral presentation. Also, many of the quotes in the book can provide a vantage point from which to think creatively about business.

Quality Quotes will be a useful addition to the bookshelves of anyone studying quality and management concepts in general, teaching quality subjects, or writing a book or a speech, as well as for those who just relish a good quotation for the sheer enjoyment of its literary punch and effect.

The reader has a very good chance of finding "just the right quote"—not only because of the book's sheer number of quotations on quality but also because of the user-friendly organization and its multiple, rich perspectives. *Quality Quotes* excels in

- Historical breadth
- American focus
- Source diversity
- Content coverage

Historically, the book spans roughly 28 centuries. The oldest source is Homer, the semi-legendary Greek epic poet, who lived in the 8th century B.C. The breath of coverage of the book spans (the centuries indicated refer to year of birth): Lao-tzu (7th B.C.), Confucius (6th B.C.), Sophocles (5th B.C..), Aristotle (4th B.C..), Archimedes (3rd B.C.), Cicero (2nd B.C.), Virgil (1st B.C.), Seneca (1st A.D.), Saint Augustine (4th), the Koran (Muhammad, 6th), Dante (13th), Chaucer (14th), William Shakespeare (16th), Sir Isaac Newton (17th), Napoleon Bonaparte (18th), Albert Einstein (19th), and John F. Kennedy (20th).

The main focus is on North American sources: philosophers (George Santayana, H. D. Thoreau), economists (J. K. Galbraith, Paul Samuelson), poets (Longfellow, Poe), presidents (Thomas Jefferson, Franklin D. Roosevelt, Ronald Reagan), business leaders (Henry Ford, Sam Walton, Lee Iacocca), show-business personalities (Walt Disney, W. C. Fields), and inventors (Frank Lloyd Wright, Thomas Edison), to name just a few.

The international flavor of *Quality Quotes* is represented by contributors from 17 foreign countries: Greece (Plato, Socrates), Germany (Goethe, Hegel), Italy (Dante, Michelangelo), England (Charles Dickens, Margaret Thatcher), Lebanon (Kahlil Gibran), Scotland (R. L. Stevenson, David Hume), Russia (Leo Tolstoy, Nikita Khruschev), Australia (Germaine Greer), France (Louis Pasteur, Pascal), China (Mao Tse Tung), Spain (Cervantes), Japan (Konosuke Matsushita), Switzerland (C. Jung, César Ritz), Denmark (S. Kierkegaard), India (R. Tagore), Sweden (C. Linnaeus), and Ireland (Oscar Wilde, G. B. Shaw).

From another perspective, *Quality Quotes* casts an extremely wide net for sources, ranging from the solid, diverse backgrounds of 16 Nobel Prize winners (Kipling, Yeats, Shaw, Bergson, Thomas Mann, Bertrand Russell, Boris Pasternak, Steinbeck, Sartre, Pavlov, Tagore, Einstein, W. Heisenberg, Martin Luther King Jr., Samuelson, Kissinger) to the more popular sources such as the Seven Dwarfs (from the Disney movie *Snow White*), Pogo, David Crockett, Cole Porter, Sherlock Holmes (Sir A. C. Doyle), and Yogi Berra.

Moreover, *Quality Quotes* offers a comprehensive coverage of topics concerned with quality. The more than 1500 quotes on 36 quality items cover the subject from virtually every angle: customer satisfaction, leadership, cost of poor quality, kaizen, Big Q, total quality management, the Juran Trilogy®, teamwork, voice of the customer, individual development, management by facts, empowerment, employee involvement, problem solving, statistical thinking, and many others.

Finally, readers in the late 1990s, sensitive to the efforts by current writers to make pronouns and other references less male oriented, will note that this was not always the case. In most instances, throughout *Quality Quotes*, for the pronoun "he," "he or she" should be understood; "man" implies "individual"; "salesman" is "salesperson"; and so on.

This collection of quotes is characterized by a very intense focus on the reader. After all, I began writing it out of a very real necessity, probably generated by the same need the reader wishes to fulfill. It is my goal that readers everywhere will find the book fit for use. "Fitness for use," by the way, is one of the quotes in the book: It is Juran's very concise way of defining quality.

Hélio Gomes

How to
Use This Book

Quality Quotes is organized for maximum accessibility and flexibility of use.

First, the contents presents the book from a thematic perspective. It provides both an overview of the range of subjects addressed as well as a wealth of ideas for the planning of speeches, reports, or presentations.

In the text itself, quotations that are from contemporary works are identified by numbers in parentheses, which refer to the reference list beginning on page 215. This list, although not a complete bibliography of sources, will be useful for the reader who would like to identify and perhaps further pursue the works from which specific quotes are taken.

The author index offers a listing of the range of subjects written about by each contributor; it will be useful for the reader who wants an overview of the breadth of any one individual's work, or who may wish to relate the diverse topics of a particular author for purposes of research. The topic index enlarges on and provides a different perspective on the subject areas presented in the contents.

Finally, there is the fascination and intrigue of making the connection between particular quotations and authors. This goes hand in hand with the pleasure of leafing through such a resource as *Quality Quotes*, using the running heads as a guide from one theme to the next.

Customer
Satisfaction

⁓⦿⁓

The customer deserves to receive exactly what we have promised to produce—a clean room, a hot cup of coffee, a nonporous casting, a trip to the moon on gossamer wings.

Crosby (16)

⁓⦿⁓

It's not enough anymore to merely satisfy the customer; customers must be "delighted"—surprised by having their needs not just met, but exceeded.

Godfrey (38)

⁓⦿⁓

Consumers, by seeking quality and value, set the standards of acceptability for products and services by voting with their marketplace dollars.

Ronald Reagan

⁓⦿⁓

Our social mission as a manufacturer is only realized when products reach, are used by, and satisfy the customer . . . We need to take the customer's skin temperature daily.

Konosuke Matsushita (Matsushita)

ᖰᘐᖰ

Since it is a joy to have the benefit of what is good, it is a greater one to experience what is better.

Goethe

ᖰᘐᖰ

Where people really care if you have a good time.

Marriott Hotels, Resorts, Suites (slogan)

ᖰᘐᖰ

All of management's efforts for Kaizen boil down to two words: customer satisfaction.

Imai (53)

ᖰᘐᖰ

We don't just want to satisfy our customers, we want to delight them.

George (35)

ᖰᘐᖰ

Because it is customers who must buy the product and who must be satisfied with it, the product must be developed with their needs and wants as the principal inputs to the new product development project. When this is not the case, the new product introduction is often disappointing.

Day (18)

ᖰᘐᖰ

High quality means pleasing customers, not just protecting them from annoyances.

David Garvin

ᖰᘐᖰ

We must take quality beyond customer satisfaction to customer delight.

Colby Chandler (Eastman Kodak)

ᖰᘐᖰ

We'll go to the ends of the earth for you.

Continental Airlines (slogan)

ᖰᘐᖰ

The things we do to make you happy.
TWA (slogan)

⟡

Customer delight represents excellence in every respect. . . . I would be delighted if commercial airline flights departed and arrived on time, every time. I would be delighted if delivery or repair service people could provide an estimated arrival time at my house, say within a given hour, and meet schedule. Finally I would be delighted if all the clothing I buy looked as good after the first washing or cleaning as it did in the store.
Colby Chandler (Eastman Kodak)

⟡

Mark of excellence.
General Motors (slogan)

⟡

The voice with the smile.
Bell Telephone Co. (slogan)

⟡

Real profits are generated by loyal customers—not just satisfied customers.
Aguayo (1)

⟡

Probably the most important management fundamental that is being ignored today is staying close to the customer to satisfy his needs and anticipate his wants. In too many companies, the customer has become a bloody nuisance whose unpredictable behavior damages carefully made strategic plans, whose activities mess up computer operations, and who stubbornly insists that purchased products should work.
Lew Young (*Business Week*)

⟡

Good service became almost a reflex in IBM.
Watson (108)

⟡

In the best institutions, promises are kept no matter what the cost in agony and overtime.
Ogilvy (84)

⟡

Users can count on the availability of replacement parts regardless of where they operate—an important consideration in a highly mobile industry. We have no orphans.
William Naumann (Caterpillar)

❧

You want people praising to others about owning your product or service, not just not complaining.
Scherkenbach (97)

❧

Delighting customers is the name of the game in which we are all engaged.
Berry (6)

❧

It is not enough just to give good service; the customer must *perceive* the fact that he or she is getting good service.
Albrecht and Zemke (2)

❧

The World-Class organization exists to delight customers.
Chang, Labovitz, and Rosansky (13)

❧

If TQM is aimed at anything, it is aimed at winning and keeping customers—keeping them delighted.
Berry (6)

❧

It's important to *take the client seriously in every respect*, especially about the little things.
McCormack (78)

❧

What business ever started with the manufacturer and ended with the consumer? Where does the money to make the wheels go round come from? From the consumer, of course . . . Success is based solely upon an ability to serve that consumer to his liking.
Ford and Crowther (30)

❧

All business is show business.
Carlzon (12)

❧

Customers Come First/ Customer Characteristics

The customer doesn't have to understand. The customer is the customer.
Crosby (16)

The business process starts with the customer. In fact, if it is not started with the customer, it all too many times abruptly ends with the customer.
Scherkenbach (97)

The customer is always right.
H. Gordon Selfridge (Selfridge's)

USAir begins with you.
USAir (slogan)

A customer's assessment of the quality of any organization is based on the best that customer has seen. The customer does not know what is technically or organizationally feasible.
Hutchins (51)

The public is always right.
Cecil B. de Mille

ᕙ᱾ᕗ

What is food to one is to others bitter poison.
(*Ut quod ali cibus est aliis fuat acre venenum.*)
Lucretius

ᕙ᱾ᕗ

Nothing is so poor and melancholy as art that is interested in itself and
not in its subject.
George Santayana

ᕙ᱾ᕗ

Do not do unto others as you would they should do unto you. Their
tastes may not be the same.
Bernard Shaw

ᕙ᱾ᕗ

The public is never wrong.
Adolph Zukor

ᕙ᱾ᕗ

The public is extremely tolerant. It forgives everything except genius.
Oscar Wilde

ᕙ᱾ᕗ

One man's justice is another's injustice;
One man's beauty another's ugliness;
One man's wisdom another's folly.
Ralph Waldo Emerson

ᕙ᱾ᕗ

Delta is ready when you are.
Delta Air Lines (slogan)

ᕙ᱾ᕗ

Babies are our business . . . our only business.
Gerber Products Co. (slogan)

ᕙ᱾ᕗ

Where only the plane gets more attention than you.
Iberia (slogan)

ᕙ᱾ᕗ

Let Hertz put *you* in the driver's seat.
Hertz Corp. (slogan)

∽⊙⊙⌀

The customer is always No. 1.
National Car Rental Systems (slogan)

∽⊙⊙⌀

We never forget who's driving.
General Motors (slogan)

∽⊙⊙⌀

We've learned a lot about food because we care a lot about babies.
Gerber Products Co. (slogan)

∽⊙⊙⌀

With the customer as the reference point, priorities become easier to set.
Walton (106)

∽⊙⊙⌀

The person into whose "In" basket you empty your "Out" basket is your customer.
Townsend and Gebhardt (105)

∽⊙⊙⌀

Markets can change overnight. One morning you wake up and you are dead in the water.
Mike Wright (Super Valu)

∽⊙⊙⌀

Service is the rent we pay for the privilege of living on this earth.
Eldon Tanner

∽⊙⊙⌀

There is no manual that deals with the *real* business of motorcycle maintenance, the most important aspect of all. Caring about what you're doing is considered either unimportant or taken for granted.
Pirsig (90)

∽⊙⊙⌀

You have to remember who pays the bills. No matter what the primary discipline—finance, manufacturing—you have to know and experience the excitement of sales. That's where you really see things happen.
John Opel (IBM)

∽⊙⊙⌀

"Customers are easier to deal with than employees. You can hang up on customers." Once.
Townsend and Gebhardt (105)

Consumers are statistics. Customers are people.
Stanley Marcus (Neiman-Marcus)

Customers, not markets. Not marketing. Not strategic positioning (whatever that means). Just customers. A "market" has never been observed paying a bill. Customers do that.
Peters and Austin (88)

It is not always comfortable putting the customer first.
Sallis (96)

Understanding customer needs doesn't mean asking customers what those needs are. They'll say only what they *think* they want.
Hammer and Champy (43)

A customer is the most important person ever in this office—in person or by mail.
A customer is not dependent on us, we are dependent on him.
A customer is not an interruption of our work, he is the purpose of it. We are not doing him a favor by serving him, he is doing us a favor by giving us the opportunity to do so.
A customer is not someone to argue or match wits with. Nobody ever won an argument with a customer.
A customer is a person who brings us his wants. It is our job to handle them profitably to him and to ourselves.
L.L. Bean (poster)

Every process in your organization has a customer, and without a customer a process has no purpose.
Hunt (50)

The customer generates nothing. No customer asked for electric lights.
Deming (21)

Customers are the most important asset any company has, even though they don't show up on the balance sheet.

Berry (6)

❧

"What is our business?" is not determined by the producer but by the customer.

Peter Drucker

❧

Rule #1: The customer is always right.
Rule #2: If the customer is ever wrong, reread rule #1.

Capezio and Morehouse (11)

❧

No customer asked for an automobile. We have horses: what could be better?

Deming (21)

❧

The next process is your customer.

Ishikawa (56)

❧

Customer needs and satisfaction are constantly changing targets.

Juran Institute, Inc. (59)

❧

The truth of the matter is that when it comes to quality, the customer has all the votes.

Guaspari (41)

❧

From banking, to retailing, to the automobile industry, the companies that are achieving the greatest successes share the same obsession: making the customer the center of everything they do.

Godfrey (38)

❧

Come to Shell for answers.

Shell Oil Co. (slogan)

❧

The customer has the money. You want it. It's not hard to see who has the leverage in that situation.

Guaspari (41)

❧

There's a sucker born every minute.

P.T. Barnum

⋄∞⋄

The consumer isn't a moron; she is your wife.

Ogilvy (84)

⋄∞⋄

The consumer, so it is said, is the king . . . each is a voter who uses his money as votes to get the things done that he wants done.

Paul A. Samuelson

⋄∞⋄

The client is never wrong.
(*Le client n'a jamais tort.*)

César Ritz (Ritz Hotels)

⋄∞⋄

The public is the only critic whose opinion is worth anything at all.

Mark Twain

⋄∞⋄

Organizations: Purpose and Nature

There is only one valid definition of business purpose: to create a customer.
Peter Drucker

Companies exist in a society for the purpose of satisfying people in that society.
Ishikawa (56)

Organizations—which, after all, are merely collections of people—exist for only one purpose: to help people reach ends together that they could not achieve individually.
Waterman (107)

[An organization is] a collection of choices looking for problems . . . solutions looking for issues . . . and decision makers looking for work.
Michael Cohen and James March

The organization exists to serve the needs of the people who are serving the customer.

Albrecht and Zemke (2)

⟡

Companies are not asset portfolios, but people working together to invent, make, sell, and provide service.

Hammer and Champy (43)

⟡

The purpose of a business is to gain and keep customers.

Fred Smith (Federal Express)

⟡

Organizational design is more like building a snow fence to deflect drifting snow than like building a snowman.

James March

⟡

You can have any color [of Model T Fords], so long as it's black.

Henry Ford (Ford)

⟡

A formal organization is a system of coordinated activities of a group of people working cooperatively toward a common goal under authority and leadership.

W. G. Scott

⟡

Companies can be thought of as bundles of skills, capabilities, and competencies.

Waterman (107)

⟡

Chronic use of the military metaphor leads people repeatedly to overlook a different kind of organization, one that values improvisation, rather than forecasting, dwells on opportunities rather than constraints, discovers new actions rather than defends past actions, values arguments more highly than serenity and encourages doubt and contradiction rather than belief.

Weick (109)

⟡

If an organization is to work effectively, the communication should be through the most effective channel regardless of the organization chart . . . I've often thought that after you get organized, you ought to throw the chart away.

> **David Packard** (Hewlett-Packard)

Businessmen will have to learn to build and manage innovative organizations.

> **Drucker** (22)

Manufacturers who *don't* test-market their products incur the colossal cost (and disgrace) of having their products fail on a national scale, instead of dying inconspicuously and economically in test markets.

> **Ogilvy** (84)

All organizations are perfectly designed to get the results that they get.

> **Townsend and Gebhardt** (105)

If you're not serving the customer, you'd better be serving someone who is.

> **Albrecht and Zemke** (2)

Somewhere, we got the idea that market share was an objective. I hope that is straightened out. Anyone can build market share; if you set the price low enough you can have the whole damn market. But I'll tell you it won't get you anywhere around here.

> **David Packard** (Hewlett-Packard)

I believe that less is more in the case of corporate management.

> **Kroc** (69)

We need to be able to trust that something as simple as a clear core of values and vision, kept in motion through continuing dialogue, can lead to order.

> **Wheatley** (111)

The tone and fiber of our society depend upon a pervasive, almost universal striving for good performance.

Gardner (32)

ᕫᘏᕬ

Sometimes the accounting people act as if they think the organization exists so they can keep books on it.

Albrecht and Zemke (2)

ᕫᘏᕬ

High-performance organizations seek not only to meet customer expectations, but also to go the extra mile and delight both their internal and external customers.

Hunt (50)

ᕫᘏᕬ

If we succeed in maintaining focus, rather than hands-on control, we also create the flexibility and responsiveness that every organization craves. What leaders are called upon to do in a chaotic world is to shape their organizations through concepts, not through elaborate rules or structures.

Wheatley (111)

ᕫᘏᕬ

Individuals form organizations to accomplish what they could not do as well or at all alone.

Wynn and Guditus (113)

ᕫᘏᕬ

You may bring together all of the parts of the machine, but you do not have the machine until they are properly related. The chief task of the organization is how to relate the parts so that you have a working unit; then you get effective participation.

Mary Parker Follett

ᕫᘏᕬ

Organizations only exist to provide goods and services to customers. Haven't we always been customer focused? For most organizations the answer to this question is a resounding *no*.

Godfrey (39)

ᕫᘏᕬ

In the push and pull of organizational life, it can be easy to forget a very basic fact: namely, that your business organization exists for the purpose of delivering value to your customers.

Guaspari (41)

❧

Organizations, like people, develop their own personalities.

Wynn and Guditus (113)

❧

A man without a smiling face must not open a shop.

Chinese Proverb

❧

Quality: Definitions and Characteristics

Quality is fitness for use.

Juran (64)

Quality means best for certain customer conditions. These conditions are (a) the actual use and (b) the selling price of the product.

Feigenbaum (29)

Quality is conformance to requirements.

Crosby (16)

[Quality is to] give the customers what they want.

Sam Walton

[Quality is] meeting or exceeding customer expectations at a cost that represents value to them.

Harrington (44)

❦

[Quality is] the totality of features and characteristics of a product or service that bear on its ability to satisfy a given need.

ISO 9000 Series Standards

❦

Better a diamond with a flaw than a pebble without.

Confucius

❦

There are no absolutes where quality is concerned. Quality is a comparative concept, and is and always will be dynamic. That is why no one has *ever* reached the optimum. It does not exist, and never can.

Hutchins (51)

❦

If you get simple beauty and nought else,
You get about the best thing God invents.

Robert Browning

❦

The beautiful is as useful as the useful. Perhaps more so.
(*Le beau est aussi utile que l'utile. Plus peut-être.*)

Victor Hugo

❦

Everything has its beauty but not everyone sees it.

Confucius

❦

A thing of beauty is a joy forever.

John Keats

❦

Why is it no one ever sent me yet
One perfect limousine, do you suppose?
Ah no, it's always just my luck to get
One perfect rose.

Dorothy Parker

❦

The good is the beautiful.
Plato

∾

The best is the enemy of the good.
(*Le mieux est l'ennemi du bien.*)
Voltaire

∾

Remember that the most beautiful things in the world are the most useless: peacocks and lilies for instance.
John Ruskin

∾

All the news that's fit to print.
The New York Times (slogan)

∾

When quality is viewed as being the number of products that conform to specifications, a company is already behind the eight ball.
Aguayo (1)

∾

Beauty is in the eye of the beholder.
Margaret Hungerford

∾

It is amazing how complete is the delusion that beauty is goodness.
Leo Tolstoy

∾

Less is more.
Robert Browning

∾

One man's meat is another man's poison.
English Proverb

∾

The best is good enough.
(*Das Beste is gut genug.*)
German Proverb

∾

Whatever suffices is enough.
(*Satis quod sufficit.*)

Latin Proverb

Excellent things are rare.

Plato

Nothing is fine but the ideal; or rather, excellence exists only by abstraction.

William Hazlitt

Thus we come to the paradox. As long as management has the conformance to specifications as its goal, it will be unable to reach that goal. If the actions of management signal that meeting specifications is satisfactory, the product will invariably fall short.

Wheeler and Chambers (112)

It is not goodness to be better than the worst.

Seneca

Goodness is simple; bad is manifold.

Aristotle

The true final test of the product/service comes when it is in the customer's hands actually being used or enjoyed. In the end it is the customer that judges whether quality and fitness for use are achieved.

Allan Sayle

"Zero defects" is not good enough.

Wheeler and Chambers (112)

Small is beautiful.

Schumacher (99)

Bigger isn't necessarily better; better is better.

Townsend and Gebhardt (105)

Higher quality costs less, not more.

Scherkenbach (97)

ை

I'm afraid as great as computers are, they cannot tell you about the quality of your product. The profitability, yes, but not the quality. The human eye, the human experience, is the one thing that can make quality better—or poorer.

Stanley Marcus (Stanley-Marcus)

ை

Quality is about passion and pride.

Peters and Austin (88)

ை

A service cannot be all things to all people.

James Heskett

ை

Quality is what makes the difference between things being excellent or run-of-the-mill.

Sallis (96)

ை

Quality is a slippery concept.

Naomi Pfeffer and Anna Coote

ை

Quality should be defined as "surpassing customer needs and expectations throughout the life of the product."

Gitlow and Gitlow (36)

ை

Quality is an idea whose time has come.

Sallis (96)

ை

Quality refers to the amount of the unpriced attribute contained in each unit of the priced attribute.

Keith B. Leffler

ை

Quality is the degree to which a specific product conforms to a design or specification.

Harold Gilmore

∽ဢ∿

Quality is the degree of excellence at an acceptable price and the control of variability at an acceptable cost.

Robert A. Broh

∽ဢ∿

Quality is neither mind nor matter, but a certain entity independent of the other two . . . even though Quality cannot be defined, you know what it is.

Pirsig (90)

∽ဢ∿

Quality is meeting customers' needs and reasonable expectations.

Berry (6)

∽ဢ∿

Anything that isn't good for everybody is no good at all.

Henry Ford (Ford)

∽ဢ∿

The customer defines quality.

Feigenbaum (29)

∽ဢ∿

A product that is too sophisticated is said to have excessive quality and is considered inferior. Product quality must be defined in terms of the advantages to the customer.

Mizuno (80)

∽ဢ∿

Quality is our only form of patent protection.

James Robinson (American Express)

∽ဢ∿

The goal in the new era of quality is to create products that will sell. The emphasis has shifted from quantity to quality.

Mizuno (80)

∽ဢ∿

A quality product is not an average product or a minimal product.
Would you want to be operated on by an average surgeon?
Glasser (37)
ᄋᄋᄋ

Quality, like beauty, is in the eye of the beholder.
Guinta and Praizler (42)
ᄋᄋᄋ

Quality is not an abstraction; it's a measurable, manageable business issue.
Guaspari (41)
ᄋᄋᄋ

[Quality is] putting the *right product* or *service*, in the hands of the
customer at the right time and at the *right price.*
Charles A. Mills
ᄋᄋᄋ

Quality is meeting/exceeding needs of customers.
Juran Institute, Inc. (60)
ᄋᄋᄋ

[Quality is] the total composite product and service characteristics of
marketing, engineering, manufacturing, and maintenance through which
the product and service in use will meet the expectations of the
customer."
Feigenbaum (29)
ᄋᄋᄋ

Quality isn't asserted by the supplier; it's perceived by the customer.
Guaspari (41)
ᄋᄋᄋ

Every art and every investigation, and likewise every practical pursuit or
undertaking, seems to aim at some good: hence it has been well said
that the Good is That at which all things aim.
Aristotle
ᄋᄋᄋ

There are only two qualities in the world: efficiency and inefficiency, and
only two sorts of people: the efficient and the inefficient.
Bernard Shaw
ᄋᄋᄋ

Quality is that which meets the customer's expectations.
Guaspari (41)

∽✧∽

Quality: A measure of the extent to which a thing or experience meets a need, solves a problem, or adds value for someone.
Karl Albrecht

∽✧∽

Quality Comes First

Quality is Job #1

Ford Motor Co. (slogan)

Always first quality.

J. C. Penney & Co. (slogan)

It's a funny thing about life; if you refuse to accept anything but the best, you very often get it.

W. Somerset Maugham

Putting you first, keeps us first.

(*Chevrolet*) **General Motors** (slogan)

If you satisfy customers, profits will increase in the long run; but don't forget, satisfying customers, *not* increasing profits, must be your primary goal.

Gitlow and Gitlow (36)

৵৩৶

Profits in and of themselves are important only on Wall Street.

McCormack (77)

৵৩৶

Customers are satisfied or not with the *quality* of products or services. In other words, the only thing an enterprise can offer customers is quality. All other indices relate to internal management. This is the first meaning of quality first.

Masumasa Imaizumi

৵৩৶

We don't make compromises. We make Saabs.

Saab Cars USA (slogan)

৵৩৶

Renewing organizations seem to run on causes. Quality is the most prevalent cause.

Waterman (107)

৵৩৶

I consider a bad bottle of Heineken to be a personal insult to me.

Freddy Heineken (Heineken)

৵৩৶

Commit yourself to quality from day one. Concentrate on each task, whether trivial or crucial, as if it's the only thing that matters (it usually is). It is better to do nothing at all than to do something badly.

McCormack (77)

৵৩৶

Customers go to the very best, and unless you know, understand, and use all the improvement tools in their proper applications, you will never be the best. You may be good, but not the best.

Ernst & Young (27)

৵৩৶

If you have world-class quality products, services and people, you will also generate world-class profits.

Hunt (50)

∽੧੧∾

He profits most who serves best.

A. F. Sheldon (International Rotary motto)

∽੧੧∾

Putting quality on the road.

General Motors (slogan)

∽੧੧∾

A business should quickly stand on its own based on the service it provides the society. Profits should not be a reflection of corporate greed but a vote of confidence from society that what is offered by the firm is valued.

Konosuke Matsushita (Matsushita)

∽੧੧∾

Big Q

To stay competitive, today's organizations must bundle service, quality, speed, and cost containment into one package.

Wellins, Byham, and Wilson (110)

Quality control is applicable to any kind of enterprise; in fact, it *must* be applied in every enterprise.

Ishikawa (57)

Quality is not the exclusive province of engineering, manufacturing, or, for that matter, services, marketing, or administration. Quality is truly everyone's job.

John R. Opel (IBM)

Total quality means what it says.

Murgatroyd and Morgan (81)

Who could ask for anything more?

Toyota Motor Sales (slogan)

The quality you need, the price you want.
Kmart Corp. (slogan)

∽∾

You can't sell from an empty wagon.
Charles Tandy (Tandy Corp.)

∽∾

The essence of TQC is solving problems connected with quality, cost, delivery, safety and morale.
Hosotani (48)

∽∾

Some people think that quality control raises the product cost. Where this mistaken impression prevails, quality control will never become a part of the company's management policy.
Ishihara (54)

∽∾

Management magazines have carried considerable discussions about the relative merits of top-down vs. bottom-up management, but to ask this question is to miss the point. Top-down management doesn't work if the people on the receiving end of the orders do not dance to management's tune. And it is impossible to get the full benefits of bottom-up management unless the people at the top are committed to making it work.
Osada (85)

∽∾

Quality is part of everybody's job.
Walton (106)

∽∾

Customer
Dissatisfaction

Despite the veneration business people express for their customers, horror stories about customer service have become a conversational staple, right up there with sex and real estate.

Davidow and Uttal (17)

The goods come back, but not the customer.

Robert W. Peach (Sears, Roebuck & Co.)

A market is never saturated with a good product but it is very quickly saturated with a bad one.

Henry Ford (Ford)

By far the largest costs that outstanding service saves are those of replacing lost customers.

Davidow and Uttal (17)

Unfortunately, the company is usually the last to know of [client] dissatisfaction.

Ernst & Young (27)

Complaints provide little insight into what the customer really wants and needs in a product. They simply reflect what the customer dislikes in the present product or service.

Day (18)

Negative word of mouth is a heavy curse. Seriously dissatisfied customers tend to be far more vocal than the satisfied.

Davidow and Uttal (17)

The only sin is mediocrity.

Martha Graham

Total Quality Management

Total Quality Management (TQM) is the set of management processes and systems that create delighted customers through empowered employees, leading to higher revenue and lower cost.

Juran Institute, Inc. (60)

There is nothing mysterious about Total Quality. It is not culturally specific; the concepts need no passport.

Hutchins (51)

Linking cost-cutting and TQM can be fatal to the TQM initiative.

Murgatroyd and Morgan (81)

Total Quality is pure pragmatism.

Hutchins (51)

∽◌◦

We are going to win and the industrial West is going to lose out; there's not much you can do about it because the reasons for your failure are within yourselves.

Your firms are built on the Taylor Model. Even worse, so are your heads. With your bosses doing the thinking while the workers wield the screwdrivers, you're convinced deep down that this is the right way to run a business. For you, the essence of management is getting the ideas out of the heads of the bosses and into the hands of labor.

We are beyond the Taylor Model. Business, we know, is now so complex and difficult, the survival of firms so hazardous in an environment increasingly unpredictable, competitive and fraught with danger, that their continued existence depends on the day-to-day mobilization of every ounce of intelligence.

Konosuke Matsushita (Matsushita)

∽◌◦

The object of Total Quality is to make use of the brainpower, creativity and work experience of the entire workforce to create an unbeatable organization in its marketplace.

Hutchins (51)

∽◌◦

An eye to the future, an ear to the ground.

General Motors (slogan)

∽◌◦

Put in its simplest terms, Total Quality represents nothing more or less than the collective professionalism of everyone in an enterprise.

Hutchins (51)

∽◌◦

If quality is not inspected in but is built in, if quality is integral to the product or service, then quality is a function of management.

Aguayo (1)

∽◌◦

Total Quality Management is not a destination but a journey toward improvement.

Hunt (50)

A TQM process is not a quick fix strategy. You won't see your competitors fading from sight in your company's rearview mirror a few months after developing TQM.

Berry (6)

A quality process addresses two separate, intertwined questions: "Are we doing the right things?" and "Are we doings things right?"

Townsend and Gebhardt (105)

By now every manager should understand that quality does not result from a beefed-up inspection corps, nor does it flow painlessly from small groups of "involved" employees like tonic from a bottle.

Ernst & Young (27)

Total Quality Management is both a comprehensive managerial philosophy and a tool kit for its implementation.

Hunt (50)

Quality management has just become too important to leave to chance.

Crosby (16)

We cannot have islands of excellence in a sea of slovenly indifference to standards.

Gardner (32)

There is no single specification for TQM.

Sallis (96)

Total Quality Management addresses the quality of management as well as the management of quality.

Hunt (50)

Total quality management is a journey, not a destination.

Berry (6)

Total quality and its commitment to continuous improvement require that work and processes be thought of in a circular system—not as a linear path of beginning, middle and end.

Capezio and Morehouse (11)

The ideas of control and improvement are often confused with one another. That is because quality control and quality improvement are inseparable.

Ishihara (54)

Total quality control is an effective system for integrating the quality-development, quality-maintenance, and quality-improvement efforts of the various groups in an organization so as to enable production and service at the most economical levels which allow for full customer satisfaction.

Feigenbaum (29)

TQC's strength is that it uses solid tools to reach solid decisions and is not a vague, philosophical preaching.

Mizuno (80)

Total quality control is not a fast-acting drug like penicillin, but a slow-acting herbal remedy that will gradually improve a company's constitution if taken over a long period.

Ishikawa (57)

Cost of
Poor Quality

Quality is free. It's not a gift, but it's free. What costs money are the unquality things—all the actions that involve not doing jobs right the first time.

Crosby (16)

Defects are not free. Somebody makes them, and gets paid for making them.

Deming (19)

In the U.S.A. about a third of what we do consists of redoing work previously "done."

Juran (62)

At least 20p in the pound is wasted on poor quality in one form or another.

Hutchins (51)

All good things are cheap; all bad are very dear.
Henry David Thoreau

৵৩৫

There is nothing more rotten and useless than an airplane seat that leaves the ground empty.
Carlzon (12)

৵৩৫

Just as doing things right the first time on the factory floor saves the costs of rework and scrap, so providing good customer service avoids the heavy costs of alienating buyers.
Davidow and Uttal (17)

৵৩৫

Each one counts. Lose a customer today and another doesn't just appear.
Hammer and Champy (43)

৵৩৫

A business that misuses what it has will continue to misuse what it can get. The point is—cure the misuse.
Ford and Crowther (30)

৵৩৫

Education and Training

QC begins and ends with education.
Ishikawa (57)

If your company is doing well, double your training budget; if your company is not doing well, quadruple it.
Peters (87)

I hear, I forget.
I see, I remember.
I do, I understand.
Chinese Proverb

Training increases skill and competence and teaches employees the "how" of a job. Education increases their insights and understanding and teaches the "why."
Hammer and Champy (43)

Say "hoshin" to the average Western manager, and he or she might very well reply "Gesundheit."

Chang, Labovitz, and Rosansky (13)

രൌര

Crafty men condemn Studies; simple men admire them; and wise men use them.

Francis Bacon

രൌര

Training is directly skills-related, but education is a people-building concept.

Hutchins (51)

രൌര

The roots of education are bitter, but the fruit is sweet.

Aristotle

രൌര

Knowledge itself is power.
(*Nam et ipsa scientia potestas est.*)

Francis Bacon

രൌര

Learning without thought is labor lost; thought without learning is perilous.

Confucius

രൌര

Try to learn something about everything and everything about something.

Thomas Huxley

രൌര

Education is what survives when what has been learnt has been forgotten.

B. F. Skinner

രൌര

Human history becomes more and more a race between education and catastrophe.

H. G. Wells

രൌര

Education is an admirable thing, but it is well to remember from time to time that nothing that is worth knowing can be taught.
Oscar Wilde

The knowledge of the world is only to be acquired in the world, and not in a closet.
Earl of Chesterfield

Imagination is more important than knowledge.
Albert Einstein

Experience keeps a dear school, but fools will learn in no other.
Benjamin Franklin

Ah! not in knowledge is happiness but in the acquisition of knowledge.
Edgar Allan Poe

Training is everything. The peach was once a bitter almond; cauliflower is nothing but a cabbage with a college education.
Mark Twain

Knowledge is a key ingredient of quality.
Aguayo (1)

There is no sin except stupidity.
Oscar Wilde

Knowledge is the only instrument of production that is not subject to diminishing returns.
J. M. Clark

Theories are attempts at explaining the inner workings of a watch whose mechanisms are not accessible to direct observation.
Albert Einstein

What we have to learn to do, we learn by doing.

Aristotle

জপ্তে

Chance favors only the mind that is prepared.

Louis Pasteur

জপ্তে

As a general rule the most successful man in life is the **man** who has the best information.

Benjamin Disraeli

জপ্তে

Big ideas come from the unconscious. This is true in art, in science, and in advertising. But your unconscious has to be well informed, or your idea will be irrelevant.

Ogilvy (84)

জপ্তে

A little learning is a dangerous thing.

Alexander Pope

জপ্তে

One picture is worth more than a thousand words.

Anonymous

জপ্তে

Our dignity is not in what we do but what we understand. The whole world is doing things.

George Santayana

জপ্তে

Training is not optional.

Townsend and Gebhardt (105)

জপ্তে

People see only what they are prepared to see.

Ralph Waldo Emerson

জপ্তে

In doing we learn.

George Herbert

জপ্তে

One can only do by doing.
(*On ne peut faire qu'en faisant.*)

French Proverb

☙❧

The great difficulty in education is to get experience out of ideas.

George Santayana

☙❧

Experience delivers to us necessary truths; truths completely demonstrated by reason. Its conclusions are particular, not universal.

John Dewey

☙❧

I am still learning.

Michelangelo

☙❧

Employees who feel capable of solving problems, do.

Townsend and Gebhardt (105)

☙❧

World-class companies realize that all firms have access to the same equipment, technology, financing, and people. The "half-life" of any academic degree is extremely short; therefore, the real difference among companies is the degree to which employees are developed.

Ernst & Young (27)

☙❧

Education is not to give lectures. It is a means of expanding an individual's innate abilities.

Nemoto (83)

☙❧

Certainly motivation and personal awareness are contributors to limiting the variability of the people in a process. But they are no substitute for training.

Scherkenbach (97)

☙❧

Quality is the target: education gives people the tools with which to take aim.

Ernst & Young (27)

☙❧

Management will recognize the need for education and retraining when they realize that people are an asset and not an expense.

Scherkenbach (97)

Training—constant, intensive, lavish, and universal—is another hallmark of companies that produce great customer service.

Davidow and Uttal (17)

Only ability and sound education equip one for the continuous seeking of new solutions.

Gardner (32)

Train everyone—lavishly.

Peters (87)

Management has to give up the notion that employees can train each other.

Gitlow and Gitlow (36)

The good intuiter may have been born with something special, but his effectiveness rests upon a solid knowledge of the subject, a familiarity that gives intuition something to work with.

Bruner (7)

Training, training, retraining, then more training, and if I have to say it again then you just don't get it.

Peters (87)

Training turns good intentions into good results.

Berry (6)

Management has a tendency to believe that when people have completed training, they are "trained."

Gitlow and Gitlow (36)

There is nothing training cannot do. Nothing is above its reach. It can turn bad morals to good; it can destroy bad principles and recreate good ones; it can lift men to angelship.

Mark Twain

∾৹ৈ৹

Whatever humans have learned had to be learned as a consequence only of trial and error experience. Humans have learned only through mistakes.

Buckminster Fuller

∾৹ৈ৹

People don't automatically know how to solve problems as a group, reach consensus decisions, or make presentations of ideas. Until their skills improve to the point where they feel comfortable, they will avoid performing these tasks at all costs.

Wellins, Byham, and Wilson (110)

∾৹ৈ৹

There is no substitute for knowledge.

Deming (21)

∾৹ৈ৹

A good theory is the vehicle not only for understanding a phenomenon now but also for remembering it tomorrow.

Bruner (7)

∾৹ৈ৹

Theory is a window into the world.

Deming (21)

∾৹ৈ৹

Earn a reputation for training your people well and you'll not only make more productive use of your time but you'll end up with the most productive people. The star performers will gravitate toward you.

McCormack (78)

∾৹ৈ৹

If you teach a man anything, he will never learn.

Bernard Shaw

∾৹ৈ৹

Corporations don't want employees who are window watchers. People who stay in one place and do the same thing every day for 35 years, without continuously re-educating themselves, are obsolete.

A. William Wiggenhorn (Motorola University)

∾৹ৈ৹

The first object of any act of learning, over and beyond the pleasure it may give, is that it should serve us in the future. Learning should not only take us somewhere, it should allow us later to go further more easily.

Bruner (7)

Experience is the teacher of fools.

Livy

To most men, experience is like the stern lights of a ship, which illuminate only the track it has passed.

S. T. Coleridge

Nothing in education is so astonishing as the amount of ignorance it accumulates in the form of inert facts.

Henry Brooks Adams

Standards/
Standardization

Without a standard there is no logical basis for making a decision or taking action.

Juran (63)

A company that claims that it cannot standardize and must rely on experience is a company without technology.

Ishikawa (57)

The Japanese perception of management boils down to one precept: maintain and improve standards.

Imai (53)

Standards should not last forever.

Nakamura (82)

Standardization is one of the cornerstones of continuous improvement.
The starting point for any improvement effort is knowing where the
process stands now.
                           Ernst & Young (27)

Standardization should be optimistic: There is always room for
improvement and a better future.
                             Nakamura (82)

Life would be substantially more difficult without standards.
                              Aguayo (1)

[If the standards] cannot be observed, there is no meaning in having them.
                             Nemoto (83)

Problem-consciousness and skill in analyzing problems are "musts" for
effective standardization.
                             Nakamura (82)

If you raise your standards but don't really believe you can meet them,
you've already sabotaged yourself.
                             Robbins (94)

There can be no improvements where there are no standards.
                              Imai (53)

Problem-consciousness is the starting point for standardization.
                             Nakamura (82)

Standards must be observed, but they are only the starting points for
further improvements.
                             Nakamura (82)

Only when standards are maintained can you expect to make good, reliable products inexpensively and quickly.

Nakamura (82)

જ⊙ન

For Kaizen, standards exist only to be superseded by better standards.

Imai (53)

જ⊙ન

Perfect standards do not exist at any company. Conditions always change, and standards must follow suit.

Nakamura (82)

જ⊙ન

Motivation

When it comes to making the place run, motivation is everything.

Iacocca (52)

Whistle while you work.

The Seven Dwarfs

Man lives by bread alone, when there is no bread.

McGregor (79)

Leaders don't invent motivation in their followers, they unlock it.

Gardner (32)

Given a choice, most people opt for pursuing a lofty goal, not only in times of crisis but at all times.

Senge (101)

Performance will matter to the individual if rewards are dependent on performance.

Baker (4)

"Motivation" can be defined as "getting results through people" or "getting the best out of people." The second definition is slightly preferable, since "the best" which people can offer is not necessarily synonymous with "the results" which we might initially want from them.

Everard and Morris (28)

I can live for two months on a good compliment.

Mark Twain

The real "bottom line" is the sense of pride and personal satisfaction that comes to people who know they've done a good job.

Philip Caldwell (Ford)

Employees at all levels will perform measurably better if they know how they are performing.

Baker (4)

By asking for the impossible we obtain the best possible.

Italian Proverb

It is the first of all problems for a man to find what kind of work he is to do in this universe.

Thomas Carlyle

I cannot recall any TQM company that did not set up a scheme for awarding prizes and in-house recognition for those who substantially improve their quality and performance.

Allan Sayle

Man is a stubborn seeker of meaning.
John Gardner (32)

∾◠◡◠∾

[Transforming leadership] occurs when one or more persons *engage* with others in such a way that leaders and followers raise one another to higher levels of motivation and morality.
Burns (9)

∾◠◡◠∾

Whenever individuals become attached to an organization or a way of doing things as persons rather than as technicians, the result is a prizing of the device for its own sake. From the standpoint of the committed person, the organization is changed from an expendable tool into a valued source of personal satisfaction.
Selznick (100)

∾◠◡◠∾

I feel that in general terms [the HP way] is the policies and actions that flow from the belief that men and women want to do a good job, a creative job, and that if they are provided with the proper environment they will do so.
Hewlett and Packard (47)

∾◠◡◠∾

We are an intelligent species and the use of our intelligence quite properly gives us pleasure. In this respect the brain is like a muscle. When it is in use we feel very good.
Carl Sagan

∾◠◡◠∾

No team arises without a performance challenge that is meaningful to those involved.
Katzenbach and Smith (67)

∾◠◡◠∾

In order that people may be happy in their work, these three things are needed: They must be fit for it. They must not do too much of it. And they must have a sense of success in it.
John Ruskin

∾◠◡◠∾

Be happy at your work.
Mao Tse Tung

∾◠◡◠∾

Surprise *is* the only route to discovery, the only path we can take if we're to search out the important principles that can govern our work. The dance of this universe extends to all the relationships we have. Knowing the steps ahead of time is not important; being willing to engage with the music and move freely onto the dance floor is what's key.

Wheatley (111)

People, deprived of opportunities to satisfy at work the needs which are now important to them, behave exactly as we might predict—with indolence, passivity, unwillingness to accept responsibility, resistance to change, willingness to follow the demagogue, unreasonable demands for economic benefits. It would seem that we may be caught in a web of our own weaving.

McGregor (79)

There is little chance that your customers will be excited about your products or services unless your workers are.

Ernst & Young (27)

84 per cent of the workers believe they would work harder if they could participate in management decisions.

Michael MacCoby

To be heard is more important to employees than to receive a $10 or $20 award for suggestions.

Nemoto (83)

The more [a guy] feels he has set his own goals, the more likely it is that he'll go right through a brick wall in order to reach them.

Iacocca (52)

No incentive is quite so effective as the prospect of having to live with the result of one's work.

Hammer and Champy (43)

A satisfied need is not a motivator of behavior.

McGregor (79)

When there is a genuine vision (as opposed to the all-too-familiar "vision statement"), people excel and learn, not because they are told to, but because they want to.

Senge (101)

⁕

The hunger for performance is far more important to team success than team-building exercises, special incentives, or team leaders with ideal profiles.

Katzenbach and Smith (67)

⁕

We have learned that there is no direct correlation between employee satisfaction and productivity.

McGregor (79)

⁕

Real teams are much more likely to flourish if leaders aim their sights on performance results than [if they] balance the needs of customers, employees, and shareholders.

Katzenbach and Smith (67)

⁕

My vision is not what's important to you. The only vision that motivates you is your vision.

Bill O'Brien (Hanover Insurance)

⁕

Satisfied employees help create satisfied customers.

Capezio and Morehouse (11)

⁕

Teams thrive on performance challenges; they flounder without them.

Katzenbach and Smith (67)

⁕

I can tell where my own shoe pinches me.

Cervantes

⁕

In essence, people do things because they want to, not just because they have to.

Buchholz and Roth (8)

⁕

Being on the tightrope is living; everything else is waiting.
Karl Wallenda

ᙢᕮᕠ

Peak performers want more than merely to win the next game. They see all the way to the championship. They have a long-range goal that inspires commitment and action.
Garfield (33)

ᙢᕮᕠ

Any system of rewards that is perceived by the workers as unfair will create bitterness and resentment.
Glasser (37)

ᙢᕮᕠ

As commitment increases, employees still give you time, but they also begin to give you their *energy*. They continue to produce (to do what they are told), and they also *perform* (do more than they have to).
Buchholz and Roth (8)

ᙢᕮᕠ

There is a lack of congruence between the needs of healthy individuals and the demands of the formal organizations.
Argyris (3)

ᙢᕮᕠ

Workaholics are addicted to activity; super-achievers are committed to results.
Garfield (33)

ᙢᕮᕠ

For workers . . . to do quality work, they must be managed in a way that convinces them that the work they are asked to do satisfies their needs. The more it does, the harder they will work.
Glasser (37)

ᙢᕮᕠ

Most people want more control over their work situations.
Wynn and Guditus (113)

ᙢᕮᕠ

Individuals who rank high in the extent to which they see their personal
goals as being integrated with the organization's objectives also tend to
rank high in their motivation to come to work and to work hard, in
their satisfaction with the organization and their job in it, and their
feelings of loyalty to the organization and commitment to its success.

Jon Barrett

If you tell people where to go, but not how to get there, you'll be
amazed at the results.

General George Patton

If we are interested in what *actually* motivates us, and not in what has,
will or might motivate us, then a satisfied need is not a motivator. It
must be considered for all practical purposes simply not to exist, to have
disappeared.

Maslow (75)

The possibility of pride of workmanship means more to the production
worker than gymnasiums, tennis courts, and recreational areas.

Deming (19)

When we ask what humans want of life, we deal with their very essence.

Maslow (75)

Cash is by no means the only currency in business. There is much to be
said for a job well done, the respect of others, or the thrill of building
something from nothing. Pursue these goals as well and let the profits
follow.

McCormack (78)

There seems to be less opposition than we thought between the stern
voice of duty and the gay call to pleasure. At the highest level of living
(i.e., of Being), duty *is* pleasure, one's "work" is loved, and there is no
difference between working and vacationing.

Maslow (75)

I have never found that pay and pay alone would either bring together or hold good people. I think it was the game itself.

Harvey S. Firestone (Firestone Tire and Rubber Company)

∾◎∽

A favorite story at management meetings is that of the three stonecutters who were asked what they were doing. The first replied: "I am making a living." The second kept on hammering while he said: "I am doing the best job of stonecutting in the entire country." The third one looked up with a visionary gleam in his eyes and said: "I am building a cathedral."

Peter Drucker

∾◎∽

Obviously the most beautiful fate, the most wonderful good fortune that can happen to any human being, is to be paid for doing that which he passionately loves to do.

Maslow (76)

∾◎∽

The man who does not get a certain satisfaction out of his day's work is losing the best part of his pay.

Ford and Crowther (30)

∾◎∽

Making money is the result, not the means, of a strong corporate culture. Employees will commit themselves fully to a company where values transcend the bottom line.

McCormack (78)

∾◎∽

The art of pleasing consists in being pleased.

William Hazlitt

∾◎∽

The deepest principle in human nature is the craving to be appreciated.

McCormack (77)

∾◎∽

One cannot have morale without cleanliness. We tolerate makeshift cleanliness no more than makeshift methods.

Ford and Crowther (30)

∾◎∽

Systems Deficiencies

Garbage in, garbage out.

Anonymous

In the early days of *The New Yorker*, the offices were so small and sparsely furnished that Dorothy Parker preferred to spend her days at a nearby coffee shop. One day, the editor found her sitting there. "Why aren't you upstairs working?" demanded Harold Ross. "Someone was using the pencil," Mrs. Parker explained.

Hay (46)

There are some people who utilize their computers to do the kind of work which no longer needs to be done. If it is performed as their own hobby, that is perfectly fine, but it must not be done on company time.

Nemoto (83)

Let each man do his best.

William Shakespeare

⟩∞⟨

If anything can go wrong, it will.

Anonymous

⟩∞⟨

The environment that the organization worries about is put there by the organization.

Weick (109)

⟩∞⟨

The people don't need to change, the process needs to be changed.

Stratton (102)

⟩∞⟨

If any project is conducted in the same manner as it was three years earlier, then you can be sure that there is waste.

Nemoto (83)

⟩∞⟨

Managers . . . must own up to their responsibility and must realize that the systems that they created and perpetuate cause approximately 85 percent of the problems. NOTHING can be done about these problems unless there is a change in the system.

Gitlow and Gitlow (36)

⟩∞⟨

Systems thinking shows us that there is no outside; that you and the cause of your problems are part of a single system.

Senge (101)

⟩∞⟨

The problem is not the people, it is the system.

Scherkenbach (97)

⟩∞⟨

Service people don't get up in the morning and plan to abuse customers.

Albrecht and Zemke (2)

⟩∞⟨

Most of what we call management consists of making it difficult for
people to get their work done.

Peter Drucker

◦◦◦

Objectivity comes with not placing the blame for problems on
individuals. Aim the questions and probing at the job. The job is what
failed, not the individual.

Crosby (16)

◦◦◦

Performance appraisal systems . . . do not distinguish between the
people and the system.

Gitlow and Gitlow (36)

◦◦◦

If you do not change the system, nothing changes.

George (35)

◦◦◦

Management is the problem.

Roger Milliken (Milliken)

◦◦◦

The ideal is the organization which can operate without meetings.

Drucker (24)

◦◦◦

There is no simple way of installing a system that will perpetuate itself.
There is no pill to take that will fix what is there now.

Hradesky (49)

◦◦◦

"Going on for years," is a confession that the fault lay in the system.

Deming (19)

◦◦◦

Horse racing jockeys are quick to say that winning is 90 percent horse,
10 percent rider.

McCormack (78)

◦◦◦

It is not the employees who cause the majority of errors; they are just unwilling pawns who operate in the environment often controlled by obsolete and cumbersome operating systems.

Harrington (44)

Somewhere in every organization's literature, it says that its people are its most important resource. And yet, when I ask people how they like the way their performance is evaluated, everybody laughs.

Ken Blanchard

The present contains nothing more than the past, and what is found in the effect was already in the cause.

Henri Bergson

TQM
Implementation

Two approaches to improvement to avoid: systems without passion and passion without systems.

Peters (87)

A journey of a thousand miles must begin with a single step.

Lao-tzu

If you think you can or you think you can't, you're probably right.

Henry Ford (Ford)

If you are a middle manager avid to begin a quality initiative in a company ruled by an executive from the old school, look elsewhere for a job.

Walton (106)

The secret of success is constancy to purpose.
Benjamin Disraeli

∽⤳⤲∾

It takes a long time to bring excellence to maturity.
Publilius Syrus

∽⤳⤲∾

Preaching quality won't help.
Hammer and Champy (43)

∽⤳⤲∾

You can install a new desk, or a new carpet, or a new dean, but not quality control.
Deming (19)

∽⤳⤲∾

Ultimate change is only anchored firmly when individuals have changed their perceptions and values, and it is important to be realistic about the time that this may take. Five years is absolute par for the course of changing attitudes and even that is only achievable if one is moving well within the establishment grain of thinking.
John Harvey-Jones (ICI)

∽⤳⤲∾

I know this sounds terrible, but I'm more interested in speed than direction. Once you get moving, you can sort of veer and tack. But the important thing is, you're moving.
John Harvey-Jones (ICI)

∽⤳⤲∾

Plans are one thing, action is another.
Murgatroyd and Morgan (81)

∽⤳⤲∾

If a man will begin with certainties, he shall end in doubts; but if he will be content to begin with doubts, he shall end in certainties.
Francis Bacon

∽⤳⤲∾

You can, for you must.
(*Du kannst, denn du sollst.*)
Goethe

∽⤳⤲∾

There are no ready-made programs for TQM.
Murgatroyd and Morgan (81)

᠎᠍᠍᠍

The golden rule is that there are no golden rules.
Bernard Shaw

᠎᠍᠍᠍

Nothing humanely great . . . has come from reflection.
Joseph Conrad

᠎᠍᠍᠍

Any new "program," "drive," etc., is suspect.
Frank Gryna

᠎᠍᠍᠍

Perhaps the hardest lesson of all is that there is no such thing as "getting it right"—least of all with the promulgation of quality.
Walton (106)

᠎᠍᠍᠍

A three sentence course of business Management: You read a book from the beginning to the end. You run a business the opposite way. You start with the end, and then you do everything you must to reach it.
Geneen (34)

᠎᠍᠍᠍

If you think you can't, you're right, you can't.
Henry Ford (Ford)

᠎᠍᠍᠍

Everyone wants better quality and lower costs, but just doing what comes naturally or what is recommended by some consultant may backfire.
Aguayo (1)

᠎᠍᠍᠍

Successful people do not listen to the voice of middle managers . . . How do top executives get convinced of TQC? There are very few top executives that get started by the recommendation of the middle manager, but by the recommendation of his friends, top executives of another company. In this case, you must patiently wait.
Noriaki Kano

᠎᠍᠍᠍

A high level of backbiting politics, no teamwork, no set of shared business values, and maybe vast business diversity combine in a sure recipe for stagnation. This is a deadly combination.
                                                   Waterman (107)

We may be very busy, we may be very *efficient*, but we will also be truly *effective* only when we begin with the end in mind.
                                                   Covey (15)

Things which matter most must never be at the mercy of things which matter least.
                                                   Goethe

There are no gains without pains.
                                                   Adlai Stevenson

A good beginning makes a good ending.
                                                   English Proverb

Who has begun has half done.
                                                   Horace

The beginning is the most important part of the work.
                                                   Plato

Nothing great was ever achieved without enthusiasm.
                                                   Ralph Waldo Emerson

Nothing great in the world has been accomplished without passion.
                                                   Hegel

Wisely and slowly; they stumble that run fast.
                                                   William Shakespeare

Haste in every business brings failures.
Herodotus

Patience is the companion of wisdom.
St. Augustine

Slow and steady wins the race.
Aesop

Great works are performed not by strength, but by perseverance.
Samuel Johnson

God helps those who persevere.
Koran

Patience is bitter but its fruit is sweet.
Anonymous

If you feed the people just with revolutionary slogans, they will listen today, they will listen tomorrow, they will listen the day after tomorrow, but on the fourth day, they will say "To hell with you."
Nikita Khrushchev

There is no substitute for hard work.
Thomas Edison

The beginning is half of the whole.
Plato

Well begun is half done.
Horace

Every beginning is hard.
(*Aller Anfangan ist schwer.*)
German Proverb

There is no excellence without difficulty.
                                    Ovid

                                    ⟨∞⟩

Without diligence, no prize.
(*Ohne Fleiss, kein Preis.*)
                            German Proverb

                                    ⟨∞⟩

Easier said than done.
                            English Proverb

                                    ⟨∞⟩

Do it and then make an excuse.
(*Fac et excusa.*)
                              Latin Proverb

                                    ⟨∞⟩

It is common sense to take a method and try it. If it fails, admit it
frankly and try another. But above all, try something.
                        Franklin D. Roosevelt

                                    ⟨∞⟩

The more haste the less speed.
                            English Proverb

                                    ⟨∞⟩

Where there is no hope, there can be no endeavour.
                            Samuel Johnson

                                    ⟨∞⟩

Slogans, posters on the wall, appearances in company videos and at
occasional in-house quality award ceremonies are always impersonal and
inadequate.
                              Allan Sayle

                                    ⟨∞⟩

Every difficulty yields to the enterprising.
                              G. Holman

                                    ⟨∞⟩

You more likely act yourself into feeling than feel yourself into action.
                          Jerome Bruner (7)

                                    ⟨∞⟩

A useful motto during the start-up phase is, "Think big—start small."
Ernst & Young (27)

∽∾

Chaotic action is preferable to orderly inaction.
Weick (109)

∽∾

Ideas are useless unless used. The proof of their value is only in their implementation. Until then, they are in limbo.
Levitt (71)

∽∾

Partial understanding of and involvement in quality can produce only partial success or total failure.
Townsend and Gebhardt (105)

∽∾

You can't accomplish anything unless you have some fun.
Charles Knight (Emerson Electric)

∽∾

Quality cannot be copied; there is no step-by-step cookbook that applies equally to all company situations and cultures.
Ernst & Young (27)

∽∾

You cannot manipulate people into doing quality work.
Townsend and Gebhardt (105)

∽∾

Just as the three most important words in real estate are location, location, location, the three most important words in quality improvement are *implement, implement, implement.*
Stratton (102)

∽∾

It is meaningless, if not obviously counterproductive, to hang up posters demanding new levels of productivity without providing people with the tools and information to achieve them. In this case, exhortation is demeaning.
Ernst & Young (27)

∽∾

You cannot implement quality improvement in a hostile environment.
                                    Stratton (102)

That's what life is all about—timing.
                                    Iacocca (52)

A good plan violently executed right now is far better than a perfect
plan executed next week.
                                    General George Patton

We believe a passion for excellence also carries a price, and we state it
simply: the adventure of excellence is not for the faint of heart.
                                    Peters and Austin (88)

The correlation between service and slogans is essentially nil.
                                    Albrecht and Zemke (2)

Off-the-shelf, canned, "just add water" quality solutions cannot generate
the level of human commitment within the organization needed to
succeed.
                                    Hunt (50)

TQM does not and will not bring results overnight. The essence of
TQM is a change of culture.
                                    Sallis (96)

The problem of quality management is not what people don't know
about it. The problem is what they think they *do* know.
                                    Crosby (16)

All excellence involves discipline and tenacity of purpose.
                                    Gardner (32)

You can't build a house without hammer and nails.
                                    Hosotani (48)

Changing the culture of an institution is a slow process, and one that is best not rushed. If the effects of TQM are to be lasting, people have to want to be on board.

Sallis (96)

⤔⤖

The first step in eliminating arbitrary numerical goals should be removing posters and slogans from offices, hallways, production sites, etc. . . . If management feels the need to replace the posters, it should put up control charts, explanations of how to do a job, or reports on management's progress toward never-ending improvement.

Gitlow and Gitlow (36)

⤔⤖

[In TQM implementation] the hard stuff is easy. It's the soft stuff that's hard.

Fred Smith (Federal Express)

⤔⤖

TQM is not an imposition. It cannot be done to you or for you.

Sallis (96)

⤔⤖

Leadership—beginning with senior management and extending down through the middle management ranks—is the "magic ingredient" for making quality work. But even a magic ingredient is of little value if it won't stay in the mix.

Chang, Labovitz, and Rosansky (13)

⤔⤖

Quality is not a sprint; it is a long-distance event.

Hunt (50)

⤔⤖

TQM is hard work. It takes time to develop a quality culture. By themselves hard work and time are two of the most formidable blocking mechanisms to quality improvement.

Sallis (96)

⤔⤖

Making quality work really is "ninety percent attitude"—your attitude.

Chang, Labovitz, and Rosansky (13)

⤔⤖

If there is one consistent lesson from those who have led this effort [toward continuous improvement], it is that there is no universal strategy for success.

Hunt (50)

⌒◌⌒

Just as passion without a system will fail, so will a system without passion fail. We must have a system *with* passion.

Berry (6)

⌒◌⌒

Concerning all acts of initiative and creation, there is one elementary truth—that the moment one definitely commits oneself, then Providence moves, too.

Goethe

⌒◌⌒

The road to continuous improvement is and must be an appropriately tailored, optimized, and personal one.

Hunt (50)

⌒◌⌒

There can be no transforming of darkness into light and of apathy into movement without emotion.

Carl Jung

⌒◌⌒

Turn the organization chart upside down.

Berry (6)

⌒◌⌒

Winning starts with beginning.

Anonymous

⌒◌⌒

The CEO of a large and well-known corporation had posted the following inspiring slogans in his conference room:

"Intelligence is no substitute for information."
"Enthusiasm is no substitute for capacity."
"Willingness is no substitute for experience."

One day the slogans were taken down, after somebody had scribbled underneath: "A meeting is no substitute for progress."

Hay (46)

⌒◌⌒

[TQM implementation] is simple but not easy.
Berry (6)

Quality improvement is a do-it-yourself effort.
George (35)

Without systems thinking, the seed of vision falls on harsh soil.
Senge (101)

It's not what the vision is, it's what the vision does.
Robert Fritz

You can choose one of these quality systems or another option or have it chosen for you, but you cannot choose not to have a quality system.
George (35)

No one knows what it is that he can do until he tries.
Publilius Syrus

TQM does not come in a box—or even on a video cassette.
Capezio and Morehouse (11)

It is our experience that, 90 percent of the time, what passes for commitment is compliance.
Senge (101)

There are no half measures in the pursuit of excellence—you have to do it all.
David K. Carr

Until you implement a decision, it is not really a decision at all.
Edward C. Schleh

Effective SPC is 10% statistics and 90% management action.
Hradesky (49)

[Quality control] will not usually succeed if it consists merely of a handful of engineers studying statistics in a corner of a factory.

Ishikawa (57)

The recipe for action should consist of 90 percent substance and 10 percent exhortation.

Juran (61)

Quality control is more than just a state of mind. It requires effective tools.

Mizuno (80)

As with many other things, there is a surprising amount of prejudice against quality control, but the proof of the pudding is still in the eating.

Ishikawa (57)

If only one or two hours of a forty-hour week use the team approach, the approach is likely to have limited impact.

Buchholz and Roth (8)

Awareness can certainly play a useful role . . . but efforts to change behavior solely by exhortation are doomed to failure. Those on the receiving end of such exhortations tend to become cynical—"Here comes another one." Many tend to conclude that their superiors are not leading but cheerleading.

J. M. Juran

It is much easier to discuss all of these wonderful ideas—customer focus, process design, benchmarking—than to put them into practice. Peter Behrendt, now President and CEO of Exabyte, put this in perspective years ago when he was a senior manager at IBM. "I was told to focus on costs, revenues, inventory and quality," he recalls. "I felt like a kamikaze pilot with a quota of four ships."

Godfrey (38)

Business Week a few years ago mocked a chief executive who responded to a slick ninety-minute lecture on the value of corporate cultures by turning to his aide and gushing, "This corporate culture stuff is great. I want one by Monday."

McCormack (78)

᷈ᨒᷝ

The theory doesn't mean anything unless it is accompanied by the practice. The important thing is to start now. Get your hands dirty. Find the problems. And fix them.

Osada (85)

᷈ᨒᷝ

People often require time to adjust constructively to proposed changes. Providing this time should not create paralysis.

Juran Institute, Inc. (58)

᷈ᨒᷝ

To be effective, strategic management must be used as a tool—a means to an end—and not as the goal itself.

Godfrey (39)

᷈ᨒᷝ

The journey toward excellence is a never-ending road. Some people, because they see no end to their road, never take the first step.

Harrington (44)

᷈ᨒᷝ

It is easy to criticize the top leadership in any organization. They are visible, what they do and do not do is known to many, and they have the power to make many changes. But maybe the real root cause is deeper than the failure of the senior managers to act. Maybe the reason they do not act is they do not know.

Godfrey (39)

᷈ᨒᷝ

Humans are organisms, not machines. We cannot speed up their responses beyond some irreducible minimum by simply increasing pressure or using clever techniques. Some things simply require time.

Juran Institute, Inc. (59)

᷈ᨒᷝ

Quality, like anything else worth doing, doesn't just happen. It's not like tomorrow; you can't just wait and it will come to you.
Harrington (44)

✎

Achieving quality is difficult. If it weren't, more people would do it, and they don't, so it is.
Guaspari (41)

✎

Japanese and American management is 95 percent the same and differs in all important respects.
Takeo Fugisawa (Honda Motor Company)

✎

We have met the enemy, and they is us.
Pogo

✎

Quality is simple; people are complicated.
Forsha (31)

✎

Well, quality isn't complex. But it is hard. Hard as hell.
Guaspari (41)

✎

When I am asked, "How should I do TQM?" I am reminded of the joke about the New Yorker who was asked by a passerby, "How do I get to Carnegie Hall?" His answer: "Practice, practice, practice."
Samuel Feinberg

✎

Without haste, but without rest.
Goethe

✎

No one would remember the Good Samaritan if he'd only had good intentions. He had money as well.
Margaret Thatcher

✎

There are as many different approaches to starting SPC as there are companies trying to do it.
Pyzdek (92)

✎

Customer Expectations/ Voice of the Customer

Expectations are what people buy, not things.
Levitt (71)

Our business is not flying airplanes, it's serving the travel needs of our public.
Carlzon (12)

If you've higher priorities than "meeting your customers' expectations," you're in a whole lot more trouble than any book is going to bail you out of.
Guaspari (41)

Beauty is no quality in things themselves. It exists merely in the mind which contemplates them.

David Hume

Ꙩ

You're the top! You're the Coliseum,
You're the top! You're the Louvre Museum,
You're a melody
From a symphony by Strauss,
You're a Bendel bonnet,
A Shakespeare sonnet,
You're Mickey Mouse!

Cole Porter

Ꙩ

Mercury. Where comfort and control come together.

(Lincoln-Mercury) *Ford Motor Co.* (slogan)

Ꙩ

Fast, frequent and friendly.

SAA—South African Airways (slogan)

Ꙩ

The airline that treats you like a maharajah.

Air India (slogan)

Ꙩ

The calm beauty of Japan at almost the speed of sound.

Japan Air Lines (slogan)

Ꙩ

No matter how effectively a company meets the initial needs of its customers, it must remain constantly alert and responsive to its customers' continuing wants and needs. If the economy is not responsive to these changing needs, the passage of time will erode its early advantages.

Day (18)

Ꙩ

We treat you as an honored guest.

Korean Air Lines (slogan)

Ꙩ

When it absolutely, positively has to be there overnight.

Federal Express (slogan)

Ꙩ

It's ugly, but it gets you there.
Volkswagen of America

෩

We build excitement.
(*Pontiac*) **General Motors** (slogan)

෩

It may be your car, but it's still our baby.
(*Ford Quality Care*) **Ford Motor Co.** (slogan)

෩

A product is, to the potential buyer, a complex cluster of value satisfaction.
Levitt (71)

෩

Imagine what we can do together.
Corning (slogan)

෩

Kids love the flavor. Moms love the fight.
(*Crest Gel*) **Procter & Gamble** (slogan)

෩

We move families, not just furniture.
Allied Van Lines (slogan)

෩

You press the button, we do the rest.
Eastman Kodak (slogan)

෩

Reach out and touch someone.
AT&T (slogan)

෩

Everyone believes that what suits him is the right thing to do.
Goethe

෩

The key is to get into the stores and listen.
Sam Walton (Wal-Mart)

෩

We've developed a term, after careful thought: *smell*. Does your company smell of customers?

Peters and Austin (88)

People do not just buy things, they also buy expectations.

Albrecht and Zemke (2)

When the customer says, "That ain't it," then that, in fact, ain't it.

Guaspari (41)

In the service sector, consumers expect and demand more, because they know they can get more.

Hammer and Champy (43)

Quality is not what happens when what you do matches your intentions. It's what happens when what you do matches your customers' expectations.

Guaspari (41)

The Voice of the Customer guides world-class leaders' every action and decision.

Chang, Labovitz, and Rosansky (13)

In Japanese, the same word—*okyakusama*—means both "customer" and "honorable guest." Disney World has always thought of its customers as its "guests"; and many companies address their customers as being part of their "family." Customers in today's marketplace are looking for the special treatment that typically honors guests—and they are receiving it.

Capezio and Morehouse (11)

The best way to understand your customer is to become your customer and walk a mile in his shoes.

Ian D. Littman

Good companies tell you how they collect employee suggestions. Great companies tell you how they use them.

Harvard Business Review

There is nothing magical about capturing your customers' *Whats;* you simply ask for them.

Guinta and Praizler (42)

∾꧁꧂∾

Let your fingers do the walking.

Yellow Pages (slogan)

∾꧁꧂∾

A kiss on the hand may be quite continental,
But diamonds are a girl's best friend.

Leo Robin

∾꧁꧂∾

You deal in specifications; your customer *feels* expectations.
You deal in products and services; your customer *feels* answers to needs.

Guaspari (41)

∾꧁꧂∾

Take care to get what you like or you will be forced to like what you get.

Bernard Shaw

∾꧁꧂∾

You may scold a carpenter who has made you a bad table, though you cannot make a table. It is not your trade to make tables.

Samuel Johnson

∾꧁꧂∾

No one desires what is unknown.

Ovid

∾꧁꧂∾

Failure/
Problem Solving

Problems are only opportunities in work clothes.
Henry J. Kaiser

To err is human, to forgive divine.
Alexander Pope

A "problem" is the distance between where you are now and where you could be—no matter how good you are now.
Townsend and Gebhardt (105)

Problems breed problems, and the lack of a disciplined method of openly attacking them breeds more problems.
Crosby (16)

After he'd tried 9,999 times to perfect the light bulb and hadn't succeeded, someone asked [Thomas Edison]: "Are you going to have ten thousand failures?" He answered, "I didn't fail. I just discovered another way not to invent the electric light bulb."
                                        Robbins (95)

Today's problems come from yesterday's "solutions."
                                        Senge (101)

Progress is impossible without the ability to admit mistakes.
                                        Imai (53)

The more complex the task, the better it serves as preparation for a more complicated task the next time. One puzzle leads to another.
                                        Reich (93)

Happy is he who can find out the causes of things.
(*Felix qui potuit rerum cognoscere causas.*)
                                        Virgil

How many "fixes" backfire because the assumptions on which the fix was based turns out to be false?
                                Murgatroyd and Morgan (81)

The key assets of high-value enterprise are not tangible things, but the skills involved in linking solutions to particular needs, and the reputations that come from having done so successfully in the past.
                                        Reich (93)

There is never a shortage of challenges for people in industry.
                                        Day (18)

If you don't fail some of the time, you're not trying.
                                        Peters (87)

We forgive thoughtful mistakes.

IBM (slogan)

❧

There is no learning without mistakes.

Walton (106)

❧

The wisest of the wise may err.

Aeschylus

❧

If one way be better than another, that you may be sure is Nature's way.

Aristotle

❧

Little strokes fell great oaks.

Benjamin Franklin

❧

For extreme illnesses extreme remedies are most fitting.

Hippocrates

❧

Eureka! I've got it.

Archimedes

❧

Experience is simply the name we give our mistakes.

Oscar Wilde

❧

Life is the art of drawing sufficient conclusions from insufficient premises.

Samuel Butler

❧

Failure is most frequently from want of energy than want of capital.

Daniel Webster

❧

The chief cause of problems is solutions.

Eric Severeid

❧

Trainers or facilitators must guard against the tendency of fledgling teams to want "to solve world hunger." If not that, they often are merely content "to move the water cooler."
Walton (106)

∾ଓଓ∾

A trust in science does not imply the abandonment of hunch and intuition. On the contrary, the history of science is studded with cases of important discoveries made through chance, hunch, serendipity, even dreams . . . Most executives who use their hunches will also seem to possess a high level of knowledge and understanding about their activities. So the question is not when to apply science and when to rely on intuition, but rather how to combine the two effectively.
Harvey Wagner

∾ଓଓ∾

I have no particular talent. I am merely extremely inquisitive.
Albert Einstein

∾ଓଓ∾

Unfortunately, problems do not come to the administrator carefully wrapped in bundles with the value elements and the factual elements neatly sorted.
Herbert Simon

∾ଓଓ∾

A manager's informed side of things is fed from two sources: left-brain analysis and right-brain intuition.
Waterman (107)

∾ଓଓ∾

The way we see the problem is the problem.
Covey (15)

∾ଓଓ∾

The significant problems we face cannot be solved at the same level of thinking we were at when we created them.
Albert Einstein

∾ଓଓ∾

Success is on the far side of failure.
Thomas Watson (IBM)

∾ଓଓ∾

Love truth but pardon error.

Voltaire

∞

There can be no freedom without the freedom to fail.

Eric Hofer

∞

There are some remedies worse than the disease.

Publilius Syrus

∞

He is always right who suspects that he makes mistakes.

Spanish Proverb

∞

It is the true nature of mankind to learn from mistakes, not from example.

Fred Hoyle

∞

A life spent in making mistakes is not only more honorable but more useful than a life spent doing nothing.

Bernard Shaw

∞

Mistakes live in the neighborhood of truth and therefore delude us.

Rabindranath Tagore

∞

Those who cannot remember the past are condemned to repeat it.

George Santayana

∞

The time to repair the roof is when the sun is shining.

John F. Kennedy

∞

All progress is precarious, and the solution of one problem brings us face to face with another solution.

Martin Luther King Jr.

∞

It is the first duty of a hypothesis to be intelligible.

Thomas Huxley

∞

Cause and effect are two sides of one fact.
Ralph Waldo Emerson

It requires a very unusual mind to undertake the analysis of the obvious.
Alfred North Whitehead

If we can really understand the problem, the answer will come out of it, because the answer is not separate from the problem.
Jiddu Krishnamurti

It isn't that they can't see the solution. It is that they can't see the problem.
G. K. Chesterton

Don't cross the bridge until you get to it.
English Proverb

The most important events are often determined by very trivial causes.
Cicero

The first step toward cure is to know what the disease is.
(*Ad sanitatem gradus est novisse morbum.*)
Latin Proverb

There is one basic cause of all effects.
Giordano Bruno

The knowledge of an effect depends on and involves the knowledge of a cause.
Baruch Spinoza

Cause and effect, means and ends, seed and fruit, cannot be severed; for the effect already blooms in the cause, the end preexists in the means, the fruit in the seed.
Ralph Waldo Emerson

Every effect becomes a cause.
Budhist Maxim
☙

The cause being taken away, the effect is removed.
(*Sublata causa, tollitur effectus.*)
Latin Proverb
☙

The best way out of a difficulty is through it.
Anonymous
☙

To err is human.
(*Humanum est errare.*)
Seneca
☙

Who errs and amends, to God himself commends.
Cervantes
☙

Error is always in haste.
Thomas Fuller
☙

Rivers rush to the ocean no faster than man rushes into error.
Voltaire
☙

The greatest of faults is to be conscious of none.
Thomas Carlyle
☙

An old error is always more popular than a new truth.
German Proverb
☙

Condemn the fault, and not the actor of it.
William Shakespeare
☙

The first faults are theirs that commit them;
The second faults are theirs that permit them.
Thomas Fuller
☙

Ignorance never settles a question.

Benjamin Disraeli

ⲟ⧉⧉ⲟ

Error of opinion may be tolerated where reason is left free to combat it.

Thomas Jefferson

ⲟ⧉⧉ⲟ

Two wrongs can never make a right.

English Proverb

ⲟ⧉⧉ⲟ

Nothing has the power to broaden the mind as the ability to investigate systematically and truly all that comes under thy observation in life.

Marcus Aurelius

ⲟ⧉⧉ⲟ

It is in general more profitable to reckon up our defects than to boast of our attainments.

Thomas Carlyle

ⲟ⧉⧉ⲟ

Make sure you generate a reasonable number of mistakes.

Fletcher Byrom

ⲟ⧉⧉ⲟ

If I wasn't making mistakes, I wasn't making decisions.

General Johnson (Johnson & Johnson)

ⲟ⧉⧉ⲟ

You need the ability to fail. You cannot innovate unless you are willing to accept mistakes.

Charles Knight (Emerson Electric)

ⲟ⧉⧉ⲟ

In my thirty years of business experience, when a defect occurred we usually looked for "who" did it and we usually found someone to take the blame even though that person may have been working in an inefficient process.

Stratton (102)

ⲟ⧉⧉ⲟ

"One punishment deters 100 similar offenses," says a proverb. It may be valid for preventing murder or other serious crimes. But it is not an appropriate principle to follow in the workplace.

Nemoto (83)

❦

It is time to stop perpetuating the myth of simplicity. The system of organization invented by mankind generates complex problems that cannot be solved by simple solutions.

Ralph H. Kilman

❦

I failed my way to success.

Thomas Edison

❦

Problem-solving ability is not an inborn talent possessed by only a few special people. It is the cumulative result of individual acts and is molded and improved through repeated experience and study.

Hosotani (48)

❦

Don't find fault, find a remedy.

Henry Ford (Ford)

❦

Failure is a matter of self-conceit. Men don't work hard because, in their self-conceit, they think they are so clever that they'll succeed without working hard.

Thomas Edison

❦

Failure is simply a reason to strengthen resolve.

Gardner (32)

❦

People in the business world love heroes.

Senge (101)

❦

Once in a while you come up with something for which there is no solution. Then you make a judgment and accept the situation, and life goes on. Count on one or two per career.

Crosby (16)

❦

Life is a continual problem-solving process.
                                        Hosotani (48)

                                        ⟋⟍⟋⟍

Elementary, my dear Watson.
                                Sir Arthur Conan Doyle

                                        ⟋⟍⟋⟍

True problem solving is impossible with the type of behavior that tries
to shift the responsibility on to others.
                                        Hosotani (48)

                                        ⟋⟍⟋⟍

There is no such thing as failure. There are only results.
                                        Robbins (95)

                                        ⟋⟍⟋⟍

A "problem" is the gap between the existing situation and the ideal
situation or objective.
                                        Hosotani (48)

                                        ⟋⟍⟋⟍

We celebrate noble failure.
                                Motorola (motto)

                                        ⟋⟍⟋⟍

I am not discouraged, because every wrong attempt discarded is another
step forward.
                                Thomas Edison

                                        ⟋⟍⟋⟍

Take away the cause, and the effect ceases.
                                Cervantes

                                        ⟋⟍⟋⟍

Overreliance on experience, intuition, and gut feeling is a surefire way of
increasing waste.
                                        Hosotani (48)

                                        ⟋⟍⟋⟍

The super successes of our culture aren't people who do not fail, but
simply people who know that if they try something and it don't give
them what they want, they've had a learning experience.
                                        Robbins (95)

                                        ⟋⟍⟋⟍

It is better to light one candle than curse the darkness.
Christopher Society (motto)

⟡

The systems perspective tells us that we must look beyond individual mistakes or bad luck to understand important problems.
Senge (101)

⟡

A mistake is an event, the full benefit of which has not yet been turned to your advantage.
Ed Land (Polaroid)

⟡

Brainstorming—the act of speaking before thinking.
Capezio and Morehouse (11)

⟡

Not being able to see any problem is itself a problem.
Mizuno (80)

⟡

The most common source of mistakes in management decisions is the emphasis on finding the right answer rather than the right question.
Drucker (23)

⟡

The easy way out usually leads back in.
Senge (101)

⟡

Although "to err is human," intelligence is also a human characteristic, and we must never stop trying to find ways of not making mistakes.
Ishihara (54)

⟡

The first job in decision making is to find the real problem and define it.
Drucker (23)

⟡

If no problem is recognized, there is no recognition of the need for improvement.
Imai (53)

⟡

It may be said that those who succeed in problem-solving in quality control are those who succeed in making a useful cause-and-effect diagram.

Kume (70)

The worst thing a person can do is to ignore or cover up a problem.

Imai (53)

The best way to view a present problem is to give *it* all you've got, to study it and its nature, to perceive *within* it the intrinsic interrelationships, to discover (rather than to invent) the answer to the problem within the problem itself.

Maslow (76)

Discussions alone cannot eliminate troubles. Words cannot always describe facts. What is white may turn out as black. Discussions cannot settle whether it is white or black.

Kume (70)

All problems become smaller if, instead of indulging them, you confront them. Touch a thistle timidly and it pricks you; grasp it boldly and its spine crumbles.

William S. Halsey

A problem well-defined is a problem half-solved.

Anonymous

For every complex question there is a simple answer, and it is wrong.

H. L. Mencken

I keep six honest serving men
(They taught me all I knew);
Their names are What and Why and When
And How and Where and Who.

Rudyard Kipling

For there are few things as useless—if not as dangerous—as the right answer to the wrong question.

Drucker (23)

∾ᘯᘯᕽ∾

A problem is the undesirable result of a job.

Kume (70)

∾ᘯᘯᕽ∾

Ideals and Standards – Actual Conditions = Problems.

Nakamura (82)

∾ᘯᘯᕽ∾

Substantial breakthroughs in performance require breakthroughs in knowledge. In many cases, chronic problems exist precisely because no one knows the *true* extent and cause of the problem. Team voting merely produces decisions; it cannot fill in the gaps in knowledge.

Plsek and Onnias (91)

∾ᘯᘯᕽ∾

There's no harm in admitting you made a mistake—but don't make a habit of it.

McCormack (78)

∾ᘯᘯᕽ∾

For every problem there is a solution: simple, neat, and wrong.

Mobil Oil Company (advertising)

∾ᘯᘯᕽ∾

Failure is the seed of success.

Ishikawa (57)

∾ᘯᘯᕽ∾

You could use the handle of a screwdriver to hammer a nail, but the best tool to use is a hammer.

Nakamura (82)

∾ᘯᘯᕽ∾

Chance is a word devoid of sense; nothing can exist without a cause.

Voltaire

∾ᘯᘯᕽ∾

People are known as much by the quality of their failures as by the quality of their successes. So if you're going to make mistakes (and believe me, you will), make sure they are smart rather than dumb ones.

McCormack (78)

᠅

If the problem is vague and unobservable, the same will be true for the solution.

Plsek and Onnias (91)

᠅

"To err is human, to forgive divine." (Well, if that is true, we certainly have a lot of divine managers!).

Harrington (44)

᠅

If the only tools you have is a hammer, everything starts to look like a nail to you."

Abraham Maslow

᠅

No effort is trouble-free. . . . The great American myth is that there is a quick fix or easy solution to most problems. Not true.

Forsha (31)

᠅

A person who thinks intuitively may often achieve correct solutions, but he may also be proved wrong when he checks or when others check on him. Such thinking, therefore, requires a willingness to make honest mistakes in the effort to solve problems. One who is insecure, who lacks confidence in himself, may be unwilling to run such risks.

Bruner (7)

᠅

Thinking first of money instead of work brings on fear of failure and this fear blocks every avenue of business—it makes a man afraid of competition, of changing his methods, or of doing anything which might change his condition.

Ford and Crowther (30)

᠅

If a lot of cures are suggested for a disease, it means that the disease is incurable.

Anton Chekhov

᠅

To err is human, but to be paid for it is divine.
                                    Harrington (44)

You see but you do not observe.
                        Sir Arthur Conan Doyle (Sherlock Holmes)

"Which was to be proved."
                                    Euclid

The rightness or wrongness of an intuition is finally decided not by
intuition itself but by the usual method of proof.
                                    Bruner (7)

Our business world has accepted errors as a way of life. We live with
them, we plan for them, and we make excuses for them. They have
become part of the personality of our business. Our employees quickly
recognize our standards and create errors so that they will not
disappoint us.
                                    Harrington (44)

Man will err while yet he strives.
                                    Goethe

I don't like people who have never fallen or stumbled. Their virtue is
lifeless and it isn't of much value. Life hasn't revealed its beauty to them.
                                    Boris Pasternak

It is a capital mistake to theorize before you have all the evidence. It
biases the judgment.
                                    Sir Arthur Conan Doyle

The intuitive thinker may even invent or discover problems that the
analyst would not. But it may be the analyst who gives these problems
the proper formalism."
                                    Bruner (7)

When someone who works for me makes a mistake, I always say to him: "We are not gods, so we make mistakes. An important thing to remember is that we do not make the same mistake twice."

Nemoto (83)

⁓∽◦∾⁓

The best may err.

Joseph Addison

⁓∽◦∾⁓

Security
Versus Fear

The economic losses from fear are appalling. To assure better quality and productivity, it is necessary that people feel secure.
Walton (106)

[TQM programs] provide people with the "freedom to fail" which enables them to learn from mistakes and accept the responsibility for their results and for preventing repetition of errors: they do not negatively sanction people and they remove fear from the workplace.
Allan Sayle

Mediocrity is the result when fear of failure permeates an organization.
Scherkenbach (97)

In our criminal codes, there is a right to remain silent. In a company, if someone is likely to be judged for a mistake committed, his colleagues are likely to remain silent. When this happens, the true cause will never be known.

Nemoto (83)

෴

Secrecy, censorship, dishonesty, and blocking of communication threatens *all* the basic needs.

Maslow (75)

෴

Where there is fear, there will be wrong figures.

Deming (19)

෴

The only thing we have to fear is fear itself.

Franklin D. Roosevelt

෴

There is only one universal passion: fear.

Bernard Shaw

෴

Nothing is so much to be feared as fear.

Henry David Thoreau

෴

Nobody yields to force unless he is forced to.

Bertolt Brecht

෴

Using performance appraisal of any kind as a basis for reward of any kind is a flat-out catastrophic mistake. It is a sure road to demoralizing your work force. Employees' income becomes dependent on capricious factors well beyond their ability to influence. Just don't do it. Base your organization's salaries, wages and bonuses on other things.

Scholtes (98)

෴

Fear is the main source of superstition, and one of the many sources of cruelty. To conquer fear is the beginning of wisdom.

Bertrand Russell

෴

Fear has many eyes and can see things underground.
Cervantes

৵৹৵

Before getting into what to do instead of performance appraisals, consider one overall suggestion: Just stop doing them.
Scholtes (98)

৵৹৵

Blame is safer than praise.
Ralph Waldo Emerson

৵৹৵

Fear is a bad guardian for a thing that ought to last.
Cicero

৵৹৵

Fear always represents objects in their worst light.
Livy

৵৹৵

Fear has many eyes.
Cervantes

৵৹৵

You cannot compel people to comply with the standards; compliance must be a voluntary decision. Compunction and coercion are anathema in successful TQM programs.
Allan Sayle

৵৹৵

Fear is the primary block to creativity.
Ernst & Young (27)

৵৹৵

Fear is one of those highly leveraged qualities. You only need to kill a messenger once and word gets around. Everyone knows that one "Aw shit" wipes out twenty "atta boys."
Scherkenbach (97)

৵৹৵

Performance appraisal systems encourage short-term thinking.
Gitlow and Gitlow (36)

৵৹৵

There are no simple tricks for eliminating blame. You simply must stop doing it.

Juran Institute, Inc. (59)

∞≪≫∞

Security is when everything is settled, when nothing can happen to you; security is the denial of life.

Germaine Greer

∞≪≫∞

Managers can count on coercion to achieve only the simplest tasks: Resentful workers will not do anything well that is the least bit complicated.

Glasser (37)

∞≪≫∞

Role of Leaders/ Managers in TQM

American organizations have been overmanaged and underled.
Bennis and Nanus (5)

Management is efficiency in climbing the ladder of success; leadership determines whether the ladder is leaning against the right wall.
Covey (15)

I believe the leader's ultimate job is to spread hope.
Bob Galvin (Motorola)

Everyone in the company is the CEO's customer.
Fred Smith (Federal Express)

Total Quality Management depends on people more than anything else, and people lead or are led—they are not managed.
Hunt (50)

The ability to create and manage the future . . . what differentiates the good manager from the bad.
John Harvey-Jones (ICI)

Leaders must invoke an alchemy of great vision.
Henry Kissinger

Management's principal job is to get the herd heading roughly west.
Peters and Waterman (89)

Organizations are to be sailed rather than driven.
James March

Managers do things right, leaders do the right things.
Bennis and Nanus (5)

A truly integrated and permeating vision energizes people and can resurrect disgruntled, routinized, burned-out employees. It provides true challenge and purpose. It makes each person feel that he or she can make a difference to the world. It becomes a rallying cry for a just cause—their cause.
Richard Whiteley

The effectiveness of leadership often depends on being able to time interventions so that the force of natural organizational processes amplifies the interventions rather than damps them.
James March

Here lies one who knew how to get around him men who were cleverer than himself.
Andrew Carnegie (epitaph)

First-rate people hire first-rate people; second-rate people hire third-rate people.
Leo Rosten

Vision is the art of seeing things invisible.
                                    Jonathan Swift
                                    ∽౭∾

The complacent manager merely presides.
                                    Waterman (107)
                                    ∽౭∾

The role of management is to provide advice where asked for, guidance where necessary and support for implementation of the procedures whenever possible, rather than imposing things onto their staff without agreement.
                                    Allan Sayle
                                    ∽౭∾

This is our special duty, that if anyone specially needs our help, we should give him such help to the utmost of our power.
                                    Cicero
                                    ∽౭∾

Good managers make meanings for people, as well as money.
                                    Athos (86)
                                    ∽౭∾

A leader teaches with patience. A manager without patience is no leader.
                                    Aguayo (1)
                                    ∽౭∾

The leader is the one who climbs the tallest tree, surveys the entire situation, and yells, "Wrong jungle!"
                                    Covey (15)
                                    ∽౭∾

A wise man turns chance into good fortune.
                                    Thomas Fuller
                                    ∽౭∾

A leader is a dealer in hope.
                                    Napoleon Bonaparte
                                    ∽౭∾

Manage from the left [side of the brain]; lead from the right.
                                    Covey (15)
                                    ∽౭∾

Leadership, unlike naked power wielding, is . . . inseparable from followers' needs and goals.

Burns (9)

Managers prefer working with people; leaders stir emotion.

Abraham Zaleznick

Efficient management without effective leadership is, as one individual has phrased it, "like straightening deck chairs on the Titanic."

Covey (15)

The institutional leader . . . is primarily an expert in the promotion and protection of values.

Selznick (100)

Set and demand standards of excellence. Anybody who accepts mediocrity—in school, in job, in life—is a guy who compromises. And when the leader compromises, the whole damn organization compromises.

Charles Knight (Emerson Electric)

Effective management is *putting first things first*. While leadership decides what "first things" are, it is management that puts them first, day-by-day, moment-by-moment. Management is discipline, carrying it out.

Covey (15)

It has been well said that the effective leader must know the meaning and master the technique of the educator.

Selznick (100)

Effective delegation is perhaps the best indicator of effective management simply because it is so basic to both personal and organizational growth.

Covey (15)

The art of the creative leader is the art of institution building, the reworking of human and technological materials to fashion an organism that embodies new and enduring values.

Selznick (100)

∞૭૭∾

No organizationwide system should be adopted until management understands its role in leading by example and creating a quality ethic that is supported by its own systems and daily behavior.

Roland Dumas

∞૭૭∾

Quality in the abstract is fairly straightforward. Implementation, however, can lead to confusion and disagreement at even the most basic level.

Townsend and Gebhardt (105)

∞૭૭∾

Leadership fails when it concentrates on sheer survival.

Selznik (100)

∞૭૭∾

The fact that the captain of the ship can clearly see the port is of no use if the crew continues to paddle in different directions.

Townsend and Gebhardt (105)

∞૭૭∾

Workers work *in* the system; managers work *on* the system.

Ernst & Young (27)

∞૭૭∾

The task of the leader is to get his people from where they are to where they have not been.

Henry Kissinger

∞૭૭∾

The best leaders are apt to be found among those executives who have a strong component of unorthodoxy in their character. Instead of resisting innovation, they symbolize it.

Ogilvy (84)

∞૭૭∾

During the last few years we have witnessed the beginning of the
transformation of the U.S. Corporation . . . from managers who
traditionally were supposed to have all the answers and tell everyone
what to do, to managers whose role it is to create a nourishing
environment for personal growth.

John Naisbitt

The leader must have infectious optimism.

Field Marshall Bernard Montgomery

If I give a command without a deadline, do not consider it a command.

Nemoto (83)

Obviously, you're responsible for gathering as many relevant facts and
projections as you possibly can. But at some point you've got to take
that leap of faith. First, because even the right decision is wrong if it's
made too late. Second, because in most cases there's no such thing as
certainty. There are times when even the best manager is like the little
boy with the big dog waiting to see where the dog wants to go so he
can take him there.

Iacocca (52)

If you don't generate excitement, you don't generate much.

Bill Marriott

 Increasingly we will think of managers as teachers, mentors, developers
of human potential . . . The challenge will be to re-train managers, not
workers, for the re-invented, information-age corporation.

John Naisbitt

Humans have always lived partly on present satisfaction, partly on hope.
And it's the task of the leader to keep hope alive. It is the ultimate fuel.

Gardner (32)

When you don't have all the facts, you sometimes have to draw on your experience. Whenever I read in a newspaper that Lee Iacocca likes to shoot from the hip, I say to myself: "Well, maybe he's been shooting for so long that by this time he has a pretty good idea of how to hit the target."

Iacocca (52)

Good leaders don't ask more than their constituents can give, but they often ask—and get—more than their constituents intended to give or thought it was possible to give.

Gardner (32)

What are competent workplace leaders? I believe they are people able to formulate and solve problems.

Hosotani (48)

I only wish I could find an institute that teaches people how to *listen*. After all, a good manager needs to listen at least as much as he needs to talk.

Iacocca (52)

Quality improvement is too important to leave to the quality coordinator.

Sallis (96)

In turbulent times like today's, we must constantly discover, formulate, and solve serious new problems. If we do not, we will not fulfill our roles as workplace leaders and our companies will not realize their full potential. We will then fail to create true purpose in the lives of our employees and co-workers.

Hosotani (48)

World-class leaders work *for* their people.

Chang, Labovitz, and Rosansky (13)

Playing tycoon might be more exciting for senior managers than
dirtying their hands in the mundane details of operations, but it is not
more important.

Hammer and Champy (43)

৽৩৩৵

Growth is organic, natural. The best a leader can do is understand the
conditions creating a climate of growth and everything possible to
irrigate. The leader intervenes only rarely—and at great risk.

Bennis and Nanus (5)

৽৩৩৵

Leaders need not be world-*famous* to be world-*class*.

Chang, Labovitz, and Rosansky (13)

৽৩৩৵

But if great TQM leaders lead with passion, they also lead with
compassion. They balance their insistence that everyone get involved
with TQM with "permission to fail."

Chang, Labovitz, and Rosansky (13)

৽৩৩৵

Paternalism has become a nasty word, but it is by no means a defunct
managerial philosophy.

McGregor (79)

৽৩৩৵

[Great TQM leaders are] in the habit of asking "Why?" (not "Who?")
when things go wrong.

Chang, Labovitz, and Rosansky (13)

৽৩৩৵

Forget your tired old ideas about leadership. The most successful
corporation of the 1990s will be something called a learning organization.

Fortune *magazine*

৽৩৩৵

Leaders are like pilots on a plane: they are guiding the flight of which
they are a part, using their charts, instruments, and coworkers to reach
their destination successfully. First-time quality leaders, like first-time
pilots, often feel overwhelmed at even beginning such a journey.

George (35)

৽৩৩৵

The green light for team building is typically a top-management decision.

Harrington-Mackin (45)

Authority is an inappropriate means for obtaining commitment to objectives.

McGregor (79)

Leadership is working people up.

Valarie A. Zeithaml

A good manager makes common men do uncommon things.

Peter Drucker

Employees do what management inspects, not what management expects.

James Robinson (American Express)

Nothing can sabotage a quality movement faster than managers who are not engaged in it.

George (35)

Team building begins with a decision at the top to encourage, and even to require, employees to operate in teams. Lack of management support is the number one cause of team failure.

Harrington-Mackin (45)

The challenge is to create a situation where you and your work unit function as a team to achieve more than each can as individuals. In fact, the real payoff—the most important contribution you can make as a manager—is to produce synergism in your work unit.

Buchholz and Roth (8)

If management is split about teams, implementing them won't work, plain and simple.

Harrington-Mackin (45)

The superior leader gets things done
With very little motion.
He imparts instruction not through many words
But through a few deeds.
He keeps informed about everything
But interferes hardly at all.
He is a catalyst,
And although things wouldn't get done as well
If he weren't there,
When they succeed he takes no credit.
And because he takes no credit
Credit never leaves him.

Lao-tzu

∽◞◟◠∾

All leadership and no management would be as serious a problem as our
current imbalance in the other direction.

John H. Zenger

∽◞◟◠∾

The mediocre teacher tells, the good teacher explains, the superior
teacher demonstrates, and the great teacher inspires.

William A. Ward

∽◞◟◠∾

Most important by far, leaders address themselves to followers' wants,
needs and other motivations, as well as to their own, and thus they serve
as an independent force in changing the makeup of the followers'
motive base through gratifying their motives.

Burns (9)

∽◞◟◠∾

When managers empower, free up, and serve, the work unit gives them
power, control, and recognition as a leader.

Buchholz and Roth (8)

∽◞◟◠∾

The ultimate leaders develop followers who will surpass them.

Alan L. McGinnis

∽◞◟◠∾

The higher the goals, the better the management.

Geneen (34)

∽◞◟◠∾

Leadership is not so much the exercise of power itself as the empowerment of others.

Bennis and Nanus (5)

෧෬ⴰ

Using your influence instead of your position power or mandating ability increases the likelihood of your employees getting *committed* to what they are doing.

Buchholz and Roth (8)

෧෬ⴰ

An optimist sees an opportunity in every calamity; a pessimist sees a calamity in every opportunity.

Anonymous

෧෬ⴰ

Boss-management is ineffective because it relies on coercion and always results in the workers and the managers becoming adversaries.

Glasser (37)

෧෬ⴰ

A boss drives. A leader leads.
A boss relies on authority. A leader relies on cooperation.
A boss says "I." A leader says "We."
A boss creates fear. A leader creates confidence.
A boss knows how. A leader shows how.
A boss creates resentment. A leader breeds enthusiasm.
A boss fixes blame. A leader fixes mistakes.
A boss makes work drudgery. A leader makes work interesting.

Anonymous

෧෬ⴰ

Regardless of the skill and creativity of the manager, managing people depends for its ultimate success on the cooperation of the people being managed.

Glasser (37)

෧෬ⴰ

Of a good leader, who talks little when his work is done, his task fulfilled, they will say, "We did this ourselves."

Lao-tzu

෧෬ⴰ

If the executive is personally making decisions this means that there exists malfunctioning in the decision making process.

Griffiths (40)

∾⟨∾

The most obvious reason for the overwhelming preponderance of boss-managers is tradition.

Glasser (37)

∾⟨∾

Leadership is more than just leading; it is providing opportunities for others to grow and to contribute more to the overall achievements of the organization.

Wynn and Guditus

∾⟨∾

Once the standard has been established, management must make sure all employees observe it strictly. This is people management. If management cannot get people to follow the established rules and standards, nothing else it does will matter.

Imai (53)

∾⟨∾

The job of management is not supervision, but leadership.

Deming (19)

∾⟨∾

The distinction is crucial. [The workers] work *in* the system; the manager works *on* the system.

Glasser (37)

∾⟨∾

Managers who are always bawling out their subordinates but never teaching them anything have no right to be called managers.

Ishikawa (57)

∾⟨∾

To be a successful lead-manager, you will have to develop your own style; it is the only style that will work for you.

Glasser (37)

∾⟨∾

If an administrator confines his behavior to making decisions on the decision making process rather than making terminal decisions, this behavior will be more acceptable to subordinates.

Griffiths

ᖆᖇᕽᖇᕽᖇᕽᕽᕽ

The problem is not to get people to do what they are told, but to do what they are not told or even what they can't be told.

Cornuelle (14)

ᖆᖇᕽᖇᕽᕽᕽ

It is not that lead-managers are not ultimately in charge, but that they avoid making their power an issue as they manage.

Glasser (37)

ᖆᖇᕽᖇᕽᕽᕽ

All managerial activity is directed at either Breakthrough or Control. Managers are busy doing both of these things, and nothing else.

Juran (63)

ᖆᖇᕽᖇᕽᕽᕽ

When you have 100 employees, you are on the front line and even if you yell and hit them, they follow you. But if the group grows to 1,000, you must not be on the front line but stay in the middle. When the organization grows to 10,000, you stay behind in awe and give thanks.

Konosuke Matsushita (Matsushita)

ᖆᖇᕽᖇᕽᕽᕽ

The inherent preferences of organizations are clarity, certainty, and perfection. The inherent nature of human relationships involves ambiguity, uncertainty, and imperfection. How one honors, balances and integrates the needs of both is the real trick of management.

Pascale and Athos (86)

ᖆᖇᕽᖇᕽᕽᕽ

Quality leaders do not work longer hours. They do different things during the hours that they do work.

Juran Institute, Inc. (59)

ᖆᖇᕽᖇᕽᕽᕽ

Bosses like to point guns more than they like to raise salaries and are always looking for bigger guns.

Glasser (37)

ᖆᖇᕽᖇᕽᕽᕽ

You can't escape the simple fact that top management is ultimately responsible. He or she has to go home at night and look in the mirror and answer the question, "Did what I've said and done today reinforce the quality ethic—or not?" That's the acid test.
F. James McDonald (General Motors Corporation)

Had Deming and I never gone there, the Japanese quality revolution would have taken place without us. . . . the unsung heroes of the Japanese quality revolution were the Japanese managers.
Juran (66)

It is the ability to delegate which, more than anything else, separates the good managers from the bad ones.
McCormack (77)

The ability to deal with people is as purchaseable a commodity as sugar or coffee. And I will pay more for that ability than any other under the sun.
John D. Rockefeller

Achieving true quality maturity is totally the responsibility of top management in our company. Others may carry it out to one degree or another, but those at the top must be willing to go the whole route.
F. James McDonald (General Motors Corporation)

The genius of the leadership function is articulating a vision of the future that is at once simple, easily understood, clearly desirable, and energizing.
Bennis and Nanus (5)

Wisdom denotes the pursuit of the best ends by the best means.
Francis Hutcheson

Inspection

In an ideal world, inspection should not be necessary, and the goal should always be to minimize the need for inspection through the continuous improvement of processes.

Hutchins (51)

They're still laughing about this at IBM.

Apparently the computer giant decided to have some parts manufactured in Japan as a trial project.

In the specifications they set out that the limit of defective parts would be acceptable at three units per 10,000.

When the delivery came in there was an accompanying letter.

We Japanese have hard time understanding North American business practices. But the three defective parts per 10,000 have been included and are wrapped separately. Hope this pleases.

Toronto Sun

Your organization must build quality in, not inspect products out.
Gitlow and Gitlow (36)

∝∽∾

The traditional solution of 100% inspection is not satisfactory because it is always imperfect . . . The real solution is to stop making the nonconforming product.
Wheeler and Chambers (112)

∝∽∾

Routine 100% inspection is the same thing as planning for defects, acknowledgment that the process cannot make the product correctly, or that specifications made no sense in the first place.
Deming (20)

∝∽∾

You cannot inspect quality into a process.
Harold F. Dodge

∝∽∾

The inspection process is never perfect, and the goal of zero defects can never be achieved, even with 100% inspection.
Ishikawa (57)

∝∽∾

It does nor matter how much you inspect a bad product, it will not make it any better; and all inspection does to a good product is to add to its cost.
Hutchins (51)

∝∽∾

Growth of
the Human Being

Many managers would agree that the effectiveness of their organizations
would be at least doubled if they could discover how to tap the
unrealized potential present in their human resources.

McGregor (79)

The organizations that will truly excel in the future will be the
organizations that discover how to tap people's commitment and
capacity to learn at *all* levels in an organization.

Senge (101)

compared with what we ought to be, we are only half awake. We are
making use of only a small part of our physical and mental resources.
Stating the thing broadly, the human individual thus lives far within
his limits. He possesses powers of various sorts which he habitually fails
to use.

William James

Corporations need to become people factories—places that develop
people—not human warehouses that only produce window watchers.

A. William Wiggenhorn (Motorola University)

The total development of our people is essential to achieving our goal of corporate excellence.

Bill O'Brien (Hanover Insurance)

෨෦෬

What the superior man seeks is in himself: what the small man seeks is in others.

Confucius

෨෦෬

The three building blocks of business are hardware, software and "humanware." TQC starts with humanware.

Imai (53)

෨෦෬

What humans *can* be, they *must* be.

Maslow (75)

෨෦෬

I think, therefore I am.
(*Cogito, ergo sum.*)

René Descartes

෨෦෬

Man is only a reed, the feeblest thing in nature; but he is a thinking reed.

Blaise Pascal

෨෦෬

The free, exploring mind of the individual human is the most valuable thing in the world.

John Steinbeck

෨෦෬

To be what we are, and to become what we are capable of becoming is the only end of life.

Robert Louis Stevenson

෨෦෬

I think that our business educational system has been literally overwhelmed with ideas and concepts that say to people, "Never mind your own beliefs. If you do these things you are going to succeed." I don't know that anyone has spent much time trying to bring the sense of self out in people.

Jack Macallister (US West)

෨෦෬

As for self-actualization, even Mozart had to wait until he was three or four.

Maslow (75)

ᵔ◌ᵔ

They can because they think they can.

Virgil

ᵔ◌ᵔ

Individuals should be enabled to achieve the best that is in them.

Gardner (32)

ᵔ◌ᵔ

To venture causes anxiety, but not to venture is to lose one's self . . . And to venture in the highest sense is precisely to become conscious of one's self.

Sören Kierkegaard

ᵔ◌ᵔ

Our traditional hierarchical organizations are not designed to provide for people's higher order needs, self-respect and self-actualization. The ferment in management will continue until organizations begin to address these needs, for all employees.

Bill O'Brien (Hanover Insurance)

ᵔ◌ᵔ

The magic of employee involvement is that it allows individuals to discover their own potential—and to put that potential to work in more creative ways.

Philip Caldwell (Ford)

ᵔ◌ᵔ

I know of no more encouraging fact than the unquestionable ability of man to elevate his life by conscious endeavor.

Henry David Thoreau

ᵔ◌ᵔ

What we must reach for is a conception of perpetual self-discovery, perpetual reshaping to realize one's best self, to be the person one could be.

Gardner (32)

ᵔ◌ᵔ

There is only one corner of the universe you can be certain of improving, and that's your own self.

Aldous Huxley

ᵔ◌ᵔ

Men can starve from a lack of self-realization as much as they can from a lack of bread.
Richard Wright

We know what we are, but not what we may be.
William Shakespeare

The bird that can sing and won't sing must be made to sing.
German Proverb

Transforming leadership is dynamic leadership in the sense that the leaders throw themselves into a relationship with followers who will feel "elevated" by it and often become more active themselves, thereby creating new cadres of leaders.
Burns (9)

The inbuilding of purpose is a challenge to creativity because it involves transforming men and groups from neutral, technical units into participants who have a particular stamp, sensitivity, and commitment.
Selznick (100)

What gives power its charge, positive or negative, is the quality of relationships. Those who relate through coercion, or from a disregard for the other person, create negative energy. Those who are open to others and who see others in their fullness create positive energy.
Wheatley (111)

The fundamental process [of *transforming leadership*] is an elusive one; it is, in large part, *to make conscious what lies unconscious among followers.*
Burns (9)

Anyone who stops learning is old, whether at twenty or eighty. Anyone who keeps learning stays young. The greatest thing in life is to keep your mind young.
Henry Ford (Ford)

The process of learning through life is by no means continuous and by no means universal. If it were, age and wisdom would be perfectly correlated, and there would be no such thing as an old fool.
Gardner (32)

❦

No other company asset improves with age like an employee.
Gitlow and Gitlow (36)

❦

I know of no more encouraging fact than the unquestionable ability of man to elevate his life by a conscious endeavor.
Henry David Thoreau

❦

Very good conditions are needed to make self-actualizing possible.
Maslow (75)

❦

It is not enough to have a good mind; the main thing is to use it well.
René Descartes

❦

Experience is not what happens to a man; it is what a man does with what happens to him.
Aldous Huxley

❦

Man is not the sum of what he has but the totality of what he does not yet have, of what he might have.
Jean Paul Sartre

❦

People learn faster from successes than from failures.
Byham and Cox (10)

❦

All of life is education and everybody is a teacher and everybody is forever a pupil.
Maslow (75)

❦

The things which hurt instruct.
Benjamin Franklin

❦

Man is what he believes.
Anton Chekhov
ഐട

Human beings are more alike than one would think at first.
Maslow (75)
ഐട

The ferment in management will continue until we build organizations that are more consistent with man's higher aspirations beyond food, shelter and belonging.
Bill O'Brien (Hanover Insurance)
ഐട

Hitch your wagon to a star.
Ralph Waldo Emerson
ഐട

Only mediocre people are always at their best.
W. Somerset Maugham
ഐട

All employees should feel like winners.
Feigenbaum (29)
ഐട

Creativity is far more common than previously thought. In fact, most researchers claim there is a spark of genius in each of us, waiting to be freed.
Dudley Lynch
ഐട

Investing in Kaizen means investing in people.
Imai (53)
ഐട

[Self-actualizing people] enjoy taking on responsibilities (that they can handle well), and certainly don't fear or evade their responsibilities. They respond to responsibility.
Maslow (76)
ഐട

Every man I meet is my superior in some way. In that, I learn of him.
Ralph Waldo Emerson
ഐട

The Good of man is the active exercise of his soul's faculties in conformity with excellence or virtue . . . Moreover this activity must occupy a complete lifetime; for one swallow does not make spring, nor does one fine day . . .

Aristotle

◈

Whereas then a rattle is a suitable occupation for infant children, education serves as a rattle for young people when older.

Aristotle

◈

Man has been endowed with reason, with the power to create, so that he can add to what he's been given.

Anton Chekhov

◈

Mediocrity knows nothing higher than itself, but talent instantly recognizes genius.

Sir Arthur Conan Doyle

◈

What is a weed? A plant whose virtues have not been discovered.

Ralph Waldo Emerson

◈

[Self-actualizing] people tend to be attracted by mystery, unsolved problems, by the unknown and the challenging, rather than to be frightened by them.

Maslow (76)

◈

Man's main task in life is to give birth to himself, to become what he potentially is. The most important product of his effort is his own personality.

Erich Fromm

◈

Man, unlike any other thing organic or inorganic in the universe, grows beyond his work, walks up the stairs of his concepts, emerges ahead of his accomplishments.

John Steinbeck

◈

We may take as perhaps the most general objective of education that it cultivate excellence.

Bruner (7)

In the last analysis, the individual must develop himself, and he will do so optimally only in terms of what *he* sees as meaningful and valuable. If he becomes an active party to the decisions that are made about his development, he is likely to make the most of the opportunities that are presented. If, on the other hand, he is simply a passive agent being rotated or sent to school, or promoted, or otherwise manipulated, he is less likely to be motivated to develop himself.

McGregor (79)

We know what we are, but know not what we may be.

William Shakespeare

Incremental Changes
(Kaizen)

Kaizen strategy is the single most important concept in Japanese management.

Imai (53)

Kaizen (continuous improvement) and *kaizen* management are all the rage in business circles today, but it all too often happens that management is so busy chasing after this or that rainbow that it comes up with a pot of nothing.

Osada (85)

Athletes and companies improve their performance in similar ways—by repeatedly working toward higher goals.

Nakamura (82)

It is only when management supports, in both word and deed, the goal of continuous improvement, that it will begin to see increases in both quality and productivity.

Wheeler and Chambers (112)

Experimentation is the lifeblood of the high-value enterprise, because customization requires continuous trial and error.

Reich (93)

Kaizen is everybody's business.

Imai (53)

THINK.

IBM (slogan)

Nature does not make jumps.
(*Natura non facit saltus.*)

Carl Linnaeus

The message of the Kaizen strategy is that not a day should go by without some kind of improvement being made somewhere in the company.

Imai (52)

[Leadership is] the subtle accumulation of nuances, a hundred things done a little better.

Henry Kissinger

Small improvements are believable and therefore achievable.

Robbins (94)

The starting point for improvement is to recognize the need.

Imai (53)

Ford trucks. The best never rest.
Ford Motor Co. (slogan)

∞⟨∾

Kaizen's introduction and direction should be top-down.
Imai (53)

∞⟨∾

Facts and Data/ Measurement

In God we trust—all others must use data!
Anonymous

Never check an interesting fact.
Howard Hughes

What gets measured gets done.
Mason Haire

Renewing companies have a voracious hunger for facts. They see information where others see only data. They love comparisons, rankings, measurements, anything that provides context and removes decision-making from the realm of mere opinion.
Waterman (107)

A successful TQM organization [is] based on facts and genuine understanding, rather than rumor and assumptions.

Murgatroyd and Morgan (81)

∾⟨⟩∿

The greatest tragedy of Science—the slaying of a beautiful hypothesis by an ugly fact.

Thomas Huxley

∾⟨⟩∿

Truth is more important than the facts.

Frank Lloyd Wright

∾⟨⟩∿

The classic tools of TQM are thinking tools. Where measurement is used, it is an aid to understanding and decision-making, not as an end in itself.

Murgatroyd and Morgan (81)

∾⟨⟩∿

Facts do not cease to exist because they are ignored.

Aldous Huxley

∾⟨⟩∿

If participation is to be used as a tool for the furtherance of man's happiness and well-being, then it must be in a context which recognizes not only individual differences in knowledge and ability, but the primacy of reason over feelings in organizational decision making.

John Locke

∾⟨⟩∿

The renewing companies treat information as their main strategic advantage, and flexibility as their main strategic weapon. They assume opportunity will keep knocking, but it will knock softly and in unpredictable ways.

Waterman (107)

∾⟨⟩∿

The best prophet of the future is the past.

Lord Byron

∾⟨⟩∿

Change doth unknit the tranquil strength of man.

Matthew Arnold

∾⟨⟩∿

Ask the man who owns one.
> (*Packard*) **Studebaker-Packard** (slogan)

~∞~

Facts are friendly.
> **J. Irwin Miller** (Cummins Engine Co.)

~∞~

A desk is a dangerous place from which to view the world.
> **John Le Carré**

~∞~

Get the facts, analyze them and then do what *feels* right.
> **Waterman** (107)

~∞~

The carpenter's rule is "measure twice, cut once."
> **Covey** (15)

~∞~

If it walks like a duck, and quacks like a duck, then it just may be a duck.
> **Walter Reuther**

~∞~

The most savage controversies are about those matters as to which there is no good evidence either way.
> **Bertrand Russell**

~∞~

A little fact is worth a whole limbo of dreams.
> **Ralph Waldo Emerson**

~∞~

The smallest fact is a window through which the infinite may be seen.
> **Aldous Huxley**

~∞~

Learn, compare, collect the facts!
> **Ivan Pavlov**

~∞~

Let us not underrate the value of a fact; it will one day flower into a truth.
> **Henry David Thoreau**

~∞~

Get your facts first, and then you can distort them as much as you please.
Mark Twain

Nothing has really happened until it has been recorded.
Virginia Woolf

Enough research will tend to support your theory.
Arthur Bloch (Murphy's Law of Research)

Science is built on facts the way a house is built of bricks; but an accumulation of facts is no more a science than a pile of bricks is a house.
Henri Poincaré

The work of science is to substitute facts for appearances, and demonstration for impressions.
John Ruskin

Numbers are intellectual witnesses that belong only to mankind.
Honoré de Balzac

It has been said that figures rule the world. Maybe. But I am not sure that figures show us whether it is being ruled well or badly.
Goethe

If three people say you are an ass, put on a bridle.
Spanish Proverb

Nothing is good or bad but by comparison.
Thomas Fuller

To compare is not to prove.
French Proverb

I grow daily to honor facts more and more, and theory less and less. A fact, it seems to me, is a great thing—a sentence printed, if not by God, then at least by the Devil.

Thomas Carlyle

∾ↂ∽

A fact in itself is nothing. It is valuable only for the idea attached to it, or for the proof which it furnishes.

Claude Bernard

∾ↂ∽

Facts are facts and flinch not.

Robert Browning

∾ↂ∽

A world of facts lies outside and beyond the world of words.

Thomas Huxley

∾ↂ∽

There are no eternal facts, as there are no absolute truths.

F. Nietzsche

∾ↂ∽

The fact speaks for itself.

Legal Maxim

∾ↂ∽

Those who refuse to go beyond the fact rarely get as far as fact.

Thomas Huxley

∾ↂ∽

Figures never lie.

English Proverb

∾ↂ∽

You may prove anything by figures.

Thomas Carlyle

∾ↂ∽

Figures don't lie but liars figure.

Anonymous

∾ↂ∽

In everything there lieth measure.
                              Geoffrey Chaucer
                                   ꙮ

The majority of businessmen are incapable of original thought because
they are unable to escape from the tyranny of reason.
                              Ogilvy (84)
                                   ꙮ

Between knowledge of what really exists and ignorance of what does not
exist lies the domain of opinion. It is more obscure than knowledge, but
clearer than ignorance.
                                Plato
                                   ꙮ

A thousand probabilities do not make one fact.
                            Italian Proverb
                                   ꙮ

Armado: How hast thou purchased this experience?
Moth: By my penny of observation.
                          William Shakespeare
                                   ꙮ

The most important word in the vocabulary of advertising is test.
                              Ogilvy (84)
                                   ꙮ

A brief written presentation that winnows fact from opinion is the basis
for decision making around here.
                    Edward G. Harness (Procter & Gamble)
                                   ꙮ

When you can measure what you are speaking about, and express it in
numbers, you know something about it; but when you cannot measure
it, when you cannot express it in numbers, your knowledge is of a
meager and unsatisfactory kind: it may be the beginning of knowledge,
but you have scarcely, in your thoughts, advanced to the stage of science.
                        William Thomson, Lord Kelvin
                                   ꙮ

I may act on my intuition—but only if my hunches are supported by the
facts.
                              Iacocca (52)
                                   ꙮ

There is nothing so deceptive as an obvious fact.
Sir Arthur Conan Doyle

It isn't what you find, it's what you do about what you find.
Crosby (16)

The difference between an optimist and a pessimist is that the pessimist has more data.
Anonymous

Normally, intuition is not a good enough basis for making a move.
Iacocca (52)

Our theories determine what we measure.
Albert Einstein

What gets measured, gets attention.
Ian D. Littman

There is measure in all things.
Horace

After a certain point, when most of the relevant facts are in, you find yourself at the mercy of the law of diminishing returns.
Iacocca (52)

In QC, we try as far as possible to make our various judgments based on the facts, not on guesswork. Our slogan is "Speak with Facts."
Hosotani (48)

The World-Class organization is continuously bathed in a stream of integrated data.
Chang, Labovitz, and Rosansky (13)

The chemistry among two or three people sitting down together can be incredible. . . . The biggest problem facing American business today is that most managers have too much information. It dazzles them, and they don't know what to do with it all.

Iacocca (52)

༄

Anything worth doing is worth measuring.

Capezio and Morehouse (11)

༄

To manage quality you must measure it.

George (35)

༄

Organizations, as information processing systems, will tend to produce invalid information for the important, risky, threatening issues (where ironically they need valid information badly) and valid information for the unimportant, routine issues.

Argyris (3)

༄

A quality system is built on a foundation of fact.

George (35)

༄

What we get, and all we ever get, from the outside is information; how we choose to act on this information is up to us.

Glasser (37)

༄

Whatever is worth doing is worth evaluating.

Wynn and Guditus (113)

༄

Even if accurate data are available, they will be meaningless if they are not used correctly. The skill with which a company collects and uses data can make the difference between success and failure.

Imai (53)

༄

Let facts speak for themselves.

Kume (70)

༄

No measurement equals no real caring in most companies, and most managers know that early in their careers.
Pascale and Athos (86)

ᐧᏇᐧ

Quality depends on good data. It also depends on executive leadership in using that data.
Juran Institute, Inc. (58)

ᐧᏇᐧ

Measurement is the first step that leads to control and eventually to improvement. If you can't measure something, you can't understand it. If you can't understand it, you can't control it. If you can't control it, you can't improve it.
Harrington (44)

ᐧᏇᐧ

We must be aware that our knowledge and experience are finite, and always imperfect. This recognition will make the facts appear.
Kume (70)

ᐧᏇᐧ

In 1965, [ITT CEO Harold] Geneen wrote a terse memo to his subordinates: "Effective immediately, I want every report specifically, directly, and bluntly to state at the beginning a summary of the unshakeable facts" . . . One newly hired aide said: "If you offered Geneen an opinion based on feeling, you were dead."
Pascale and Athos (86)

ᐧᏇᐧ

In this life we want nothing but facts, sir; nothing but facts.
Charles Dickens

ᐧᏇᐧ

Not everything that counts can be counted; not everything that can be counted counts.
Albert Einstein

ᐧᏇᐧ

Statistics/
Statistical Thinking

Management cannot intelligently change company systems without an understanding of statistical thinking.

Scherkenbach (97)

Statistical thinking will one day be as necessary for efficient citizenship as the ability to read and write.

H. G. Wells

The ability to treat matters from the statistical viewpoint is more important than the individual methods.

Kume (70)

We live in a world of dispersion.

Ishikawa (55)

There are three kinds of lies: lies, damned lies, and statistics.
Mark Twain

᠁

Probabilities direct the conduct of the wise man.
Cicero

᠁

I don't believe in mathematics.
Albert Einstein

᠁

Believe the facts.
(*Credite rebus.*)

Ovid

᠁

Make a habit of discussing a problem on the basis of the data and respecting the facts shown by them.
Ishikawa (55)

᠁

Top Management Commitment

They watch your feet, not your lips.
Peters (87)

IWe have yet to find a company that can provide superior service without top managers who are fanatically committed to service.
Davidow and Uttal (17)

Quality service is a top down affair. It starts at the top or it doesn't start.
Albrecht and Zemke (2)

Observing many companies in action, I am unable to point to a single instance in which stunning results were gotten without the active and personal leadership of the upper managers.
Juran (65)

For an executive to know what he wants is not enough. He needs to have the will of an Olympic athlete.
Pascale and Athos (86)

∽◌∾

Leadership is where the most value is created, nurtured, and developed.
Reich (93)

∽◌∾

The risk of not deciding is often the greatest of all risks to the organization.
Everard and Morris (28)

∽◌∾

Commitment is measured in terms of visible and tangible things, not in terms of rhetoric.
Murgatroyd and Morgan (81)

∽◌∾

If you can dream it, you can do it.
Walt Disney

∽◌∾

Total Quality is totally dependent on the support and involvement of this most senior group. Top managers like to delegate, but this is a case where delegation equals abdication.
Hutchins (51)

∽◌∾

The road to hell is paved with good intentions, and the road to managerial and organizational ruin is paved with decisions that have not been implemented—or worse, still, that have been implemented half-heartedly.
Everard and Morris (28)

∽◌∾

If you don't believe it, you won't understand it.
(*Nisi credideritis, non intelligitis.*)
St. Augustine

∽◌∾

Those who believe that they are exclusively in the right are generally those who achieve something.
Aldous Huxley

∽◌∾

There is no more miserable human being than one in whom nothing is habitual but indecision.

William James

∾◦∾

Where is quality made? Quality is made in the boardroom.

W. Edwards Deming

∾◦∾

The CEO convert takes an active role in quality promotion to overcome a legacy of doubt and hesitation. The job cannot be delegated.

Walton (106)

∾◦∾

What you are shouts so loudly in my ears I cannot hear what you say.

Ralph Waldo Emerson

∾◦∾

Of central concern . . . must be the commitment not only to get involved but to stay directly involved for this will be the only means by which staff will be motivated and the quality program will be a success.

Allan Sayle

∾◦∾

Saying is one thing and doing is another.

Montaigne

∾◦∾

Only passions, great passions, can elevate the soul to great things.

Diderot

∾◦∾

Fair words cost nothing.

John Gay

∾◦∾

Let deeds match words.

Plautus

∾◦∾

A good example is the best sermon.

Thomas Fuller

∾◦∾

The way to Hell is plastered with good resolutions.
German Proverb

Unless the most senior executive shows leadership through involvement
and by example, the whole exercise will fail. It is important to get out of
the executive suite and talk to the staff face-to-face at all levels, not just
through their superiors.
Allan Sayle

If I had a brick for every time I've repeated the phrase Q.S.C.&V.
(Quality, Service, Cleanliness, and Value), I think I'd probably be able
to bridge the Atlantic Ocean with them.
Ray Kroc (McDonald's)

Whenever anything is being accomplished, it is being done, I have
learned, by a monomaniac with a mission.
Drucker (25)

Nobody will take his eyes off the income statement or put his heart on
the line without constant demonstration of support from the top.
Davidow and Uttal (17)

There are two common stumbling blocks to senior management
commitment to a quality process: "This looks too easy" and "This looks
too hard."
Townsend and Gebhardt (105)

It is easy for the folks on the top to get religion. Talk is cheap.
Scherkenbach (97)

Taking care of customers is so much work that it gets done only if the
people at the top lead the charge.
Davidow and Uttal (17)

If senior management do not give TQM their backing there is little that
anyone else in the organization can do.
Sallis (96)

Once you adopt and communicate a quality policy, stick with it, live it, and protect it. You get only one chance!

Berry (6)

⋙

Every great and commanding moment in the annals of the world is the triumph of some enthusiasm.

Ralph Waldo Emerson

⋙

We cannot afford to have spectators and bench sitters when it comes to quality.

Berry (6)

⋙

You can preach a better sermon with your life than with your lips.

Oliver Goldsmith

⋙

There's no great success without great commitment.

Robbins (95)

⋙

Genuine commitment is always to something larger than ourselves.

Bill O'Brien (Hanover Insurance)

⋙

The transformation to world-class quality is not possible without committed, visionary, hands-on leadership.

George (35)

⋙

Go put your creed into your deed.

Ralph Waldo Emerson

⋙

Trees die from the top.

Peter Drucker

⋙

If your company's leaders are merely passengers, no one will drive you anywhere, and total quality management will not even be on your map.

George (35)

⋙

Actions speak louder than words.

Anonymous

ᴄᴏᴏᴏ

We have all learned Emerson's aphorism: "A foolish consistency is the hobgoblin of little minds." We also know from experience that inflexible adherence to a course of action can be detrimental. The key words are *foolish* and *inflexible*. We are not talking about either here. Executives in quality organizations have demonstrated that they will not permit the ordinary press of affairs, or even the extraordinary, to stop or slow significantly their efforts to achieve quality leadership.

Juran Institute, Inc. (59)

ᴄᴏᴏᴏ

Change begins at the top.

Hradesky (49)

ᴄᴏᴏᴏ

Consistency in quality means not allowing the ordinary rush of business and even extraordinary events to slow or suspend the process.

Juran Institute, Inc. (58)

ᴄᴏᴏᴏ

When better cars are built, Buick will build them.

(*Buick*) *General Motors* (slogan)

ᴄᴏᴏᴏ

People watch you. Quality is in your heart.

Stew Leonard Jr.

ᴄᴏᴏᴏ

Create your vision, then systematically follow it. There are no guarantees of success. There is only the assurance that if you do nothing, you will accomplish nothing. . . . Where do you want to start?

Forsha (31)

ᴄᴏᴏᴏ

Productivity, Competitiveness, and Survival

Adequate is no longer good enough. If a company can't stand shoulder to shoulder with the world's best in a competitive category, it soon has no place to stand at all.

Hammer and Champy (43)

Service is not a competitive edge, it is *the* competitive edge.

Albrecht and Zemke (2)

Whether or not to adopt improved quality practices is no longer a real option for most companies. The only option, really, is *when* to shift and whether your company will do it soon enough to remain competitive.

Hunt (50)

To survive in today's environment of global competition, never-ending change and complexity, rising customer expectations and continuous cost pressures, business process effectiveness and efficiency must constantly improve. A top management focus on process quality management is no longer a choice. It is mandatory!
Juran Institute, Inc. (60)

Historically we've said, "Quality costs money," while our competition overseas has been saying, "Quality makes money." And they've been proving it.
Harrington (44)

Even the most inspiring trademark cannot retain its value forever. Memories fade. New products connected to new brands gain followings.
Reich (93)

The true Total Quality organization will eliminate all competition other than from other Total Quality giants.
Hutchins (51)

Matshushita's videotape is as good as Kodak's. Thus, like patents and trademarks, comforting brand names lose their value as they age. Even this form of good-will is a depreciating asset.
Reich (93)

In the past we competed in units of product. In the future we will be competing in units of time.
John Young (Hewlett-Packard)

Given the same capital, labor, and technology, one firm can produce better quality with higher and continually improving productivity than another if it possesses profound knowledge and the other does not.
Aguayo (1)

You [= Japan] will never be able to compete with the United States in technology, but you do make very good handkerchiefs and pyjamas which would sell very well in the USA, why don't you export these?
John Foster Dulles (1950)

The company that constantly responds to its competitors already has its back against the wall.

Aguayo (1)

ᕲᐧᕲᕲᐧ

The Total Quality organization is a global competitor because only the best is good enough.

Hutchins (51)

ᕲᐧᕲᕲᐧ

If you can't be good be careful.

American Proverb

ᕲᐧᕲᕲᐧ

Benchmarking means out-maneuvering your competitors.

Allan Sayle

ᕲᐧᕲᕲᐧ

If you just try to meet the competition, you will not survive in this new economic age. You must try to meet the customer, not just the competition.

Scherkenbach (97)

ᕲᐧᕲᕲᐧ

Competition brings out the best in products and the worst in people.

David Sarnoff

ᕲᐧᕲᕲᐧ

In the final analysis, companies do not have a choice of whether or not they will embrace this new thinking. These [TQM] philosophies and concepts are simply too powerful to be ignored.

Ernst & Young (27)

ᕲᐧᕲᕲᐧ

Not to think through the futurity of short-term decisions and their impact long after "we are all dead" is irresponsible.

Scherkenbach (97)

ᕲᐧᕲᕲᐧ

Today, companies must move fast, or they won't be moving at all.

Hammer and Champy (43)

ᕲᐧᕲᕲᐧ

When an institution, organization, or nation loses its capacity to inspire high individual performance, its great days are over.

Gardner (32)

ᕲᐧᕲᕲᐧ

Quality management is needed because nothing is simple anymore, if indeed it ever was.

Crosby (16)

ᴄ∾ᘐᘐᕲ∾

The ironic truth is that American companies are now performing so badly precisely because they used to perform so well.

Hammer and Champy (43)

ᴄ∾ᘐᘐᕲ∾

If quality improves, productivity increases. To increase productivity, management must stress quality not quantity.

Gitlow and Gitlow (36)

ᴄ∾ᘐᘐᕲ∾

P&G [Procter & Gamble] is a great company, and we're implementing total quality to stay great.

Tom Laco (Procter & Gamble)

ᴄ∾ᘐᘐᕲ∾

In world-class organizations, working to improve quality is not an extracurricular activity. It is a minimum requirement.

Chang, Labovitz, and Rosansky (13)

ᴄ∾ᘐᘐᕲ∾

When written in Chinese, the word "crisis" is composed of two characters—one represents danger, and the other represents opportunity.

John F. Kennedy

ᴄ∾ᘐᘐᕲ∾

The meeting of preparation with opportunity generates the offspring we call luck.

Robbins (95)

ᴄ∾ᘐᘐᕲ∾

Money is what fueled the industrial society. But in the informational society, the fuel, the power, is knowledge.

John Kenneth Galbraith

ᴄ∾ᘐᘐᕲ∾

The ability to learn faster than your competitors may be the only sustainable competitive advantage.

Arie De Geus (Royal Dutch/Shell)

ᴄ∾ᘐᘐᕲ∾

Creative strategies seldom emerge from the annual planning ritual. The starting point for next year's strategy is almost always this year's strategy.
Gary Hamel and C. K. Prahalad

∽◎◎∽

Companies can no longer expect average quality to impress prospective customers. Quality is merely the ticket into the game.
George (35)

∽◎◎∽

The company that fails to take TQC seriously—even if it does manage to turn a short-term profit—runs a very real risk of bankruptcy.
Mizuno (80)

∽◎◎∽

Still water becomes stagnant: when no further improvement can be found, the company is doomed.
Ishihara (54)

∽◎◎∽

Although strategic planning is billed as a way of becoming more future oriented, most managers, when pressed, will admit that their strategic plans reveal more about today's problems than tomorrow's opportunities.
Gary Hamel and C. K. Prahalad

∽◎◎∽

[Benchmarking] is the difference between teaching yourself how to hit a golf ball and taking lessons from Jack Nicklaus.
George (35)

∽◎◎∽

In considering quality, it is often necessary to turn your thinking upside down and to realize that quality and profit are not mutually exclusive.
Mizuno (80)

∽◎◎∽

Two shoe salesmen find themselves in a rustic backward part of Africa. The first salesman wires back to his head office: "There is no prospect of sales. Natives do not wear shoes!" The other salesman wires: "No one wears shoes here. We can dominate the market. Send all possible stock."
David Silver

∽◎◎∽

The corporation that is satisfied with the status quo and makes no attempt to grow will soon find itself stagnating and unable to survive the competition. No matter how superior the technology, it is severely limited if it is confined to the skill of a single worker.

Mizuno (80)

Companies tend to have trouble sustaining competitive advantage. Total quality, because of its focus on benchmarking customer and customer satisfaction, is basically an insurance policy for sustaining competitive advantage over the long term, even when a company might not, at any given time, have a blockbuster advantage over the others. Total quality is the very essence of our long term growth strategy.

Edwin Artzt (Procter & Gamble)

Doing It Right the First Time

Do it right the first time.

Crosby (16)

[In service] the only level we want to set for errors, mistakes, and blunders is zero. The only level we want for wasted time is zero. We should not set an acceptable level for discourtesy, rudeness, indifference, or surliness.

A. C. Rosander

The reason we don't have the time to fix it today is that we didn't take the time to do it right yesterday.

Harrington (44)

A good play needs no epilogue.

William Shakespeare

∾◦∾

To desire to have things done quickly prevents their being done thoroughly.

Confucius

∾◦∾

Why spend all this time finding, fixing and fighting when you could have prevented the problem in the first place?

Crosby (16)

∾◦∾

Quality in
Daily Work Life

We expect a lot—highly motivated people consciously choosing to do whatever is in their power to assure every customer is satisfied . . . and more. Every day. Without this concentrated effort, attempting a flawless service is really quite futile.

Fred Smith (Federal Express)

Japanese management keeps telling the workers that those at the frontier [= front line] know the business best, and that innovation and improvement must come from the *genba* (where the action is).

Kenichi Ohmae

We earn our wings every day.

Eastern Airlines (slogan)

The only way to get people to adopt constant improvement as a way of life in doing daily business is by *empowering* them.
                          Byham and Cox (10)

Difficult things take a long time; the impossible takes a little longer.
                          Anonymous

Works done least rapidly
Art most cherishes.
                          Robert Browning

"Begin at the beginning," the King said gravely, "and go on till you come to the end: then stop."
                          Lewis Carroll

Men's natures are alike; it is their habits that carry them far apart.
                          Confucius

Genius is one percent inspiration and ninety-nine percent perspiration.
                          Thomas Edison

Work expands so as to fill the time available for its completion.
                          Cyril Parkinson (Parkinson's Law)

Nothing that actually occurs is of the smallest importance.
                          Oscar Wilde

Whatever is worth doing at all is worth doing well.
                          Earl of Chesterfield

As if you could kill time, without injuring eternity.
                          Henry David Thoreau

We have 120,000 employees stashed in various places around the world, and I frankly have no idea what the hell they're doing.
                          Andy Pearson (Pepsico Inc.)

We are what we repeatedly do. Excellence, then, is not an act, but a habit.
Aristotle

๛

Habits are like a cable. We weave a strand of it everyday and soon it cannot be broken.
Horace Mann

๛

Each morning sees some task begin,
Each evening sees it close;
Something attempted, something done,
Has earned a night's repose.
Henry Wadsworth Longfellow

๛

The basic philosophy of an organization has far more to do with its achievements than do technological or economic resources, organizational structure, innovation and timing.
Thomas Watson Jr. (IBM)

๛

Never acquire a business you don't know how to run.
Robert Johnson (Johnson and Johnson)

๛

This company has never left its base. We seek to be anything but a conglomerate.
Edward G. Harness (Procter & Gamble)

๛

Eighty percent of success is showing up.
Woody Allen

๛

The spirit of the thing lives in the details.
Mies van der Rohe

๛

We don't seek to be one thousand percent better at any one thing. We seek to be one percent better at one thousand things.
Peters and Austin (88)

๛

God is in the details.
Mies van der Rohe

A little neglect may breed great mischief . . . for the want of a nail the
shoe was lost; for the want of a shoe the horse was lost; and for the
want of a horse the rider was lost.
Benjamin Franklin

Habit is habit, and not to be flung out of the window by any man, but
coaxed downstairs a step at a time.
Mark Twain

Our reputation for quality is only as good as our last machine or our last
customer call.
Frank Cary

Work is love made visible.
Kahlil Gibran

The winds and the waves are always on the side of the ablest navigators.
Edward Gibbon

When one has much to put in them, a day has a hundred pockets.
F. Nietzsche

Things won are done: joy's soul lies in the doing.
William Shakespeare

Authority
and Responsibility/
Empowerment

Managers at all levels must return to their subordinates the authority they have slowly usurped over the years.

Townsend and Gebhardt (105)

Sep

For us, responsibility and decision-making must be pushed to the person closest to the job.

Fred Smith (Federal Express)

Sep

It is clear that when workers are responsible only for following the established manual, their responsibility for quality becomes obscure.

Kondo (68)

Sep

Sharing responsibility with people does not mean *abandoning* responsibility.
Byham and Cox (10)

လ—ၜၜ—ၜ

Autonomy is a product of discipline.
Peters and Waterman (89)

လ—ၜၜ—ၜ

The buck stops here.
Harry Truman

လ—ၜၜ—ၜ

Everybody's business is nobody's business.
Anonymous

လ—ၜၜ—ၜ

I believe that every right implies a responsibility; every opportunity, an obligation; every possession, a duty.
John D. Rockefeller

လ—ၜၜ—ၜ

Being a man is, precisely, to be responsible.
Antoine de Saint-Exupéry

လ—ၜၜ—ၜ

The idea is that one can consider individual jobs as being "processes" that can be be planned and controlled. In a TQM environment much of the responsibility for planning the process is delegated to the person who has actually to accomplish it together with total responsibility for actually controlling it.
Allan Sayle

လ—ၜၜ—ၜ

Most Japanese companies don't even have a reasonable organization chart. Nobody knows how Honda is organized, except that it uses lots of project teams and is quite flexible.
Kenichi Ohmae

လ—ၜၜ—ၜ

Time after time, team members set what they feel are challenging but realistic goals for themselves, and once the program gets rolling, they find that they are not only meeting but exceeding their goals. This is something that rarely happens if goals are set *for* the team, rather than *by* the team.
Mark Shepherd (Texas Instruments)

လ—ၜၜ—ၜ

Responsibility for contributing to quality is a condition of employment—as natural as beginning work on time or attending a training class or picking up a paycheck.

Townsend and Gebhardt (105)

⤷⤶

To many managers, autonomy is just one small step away from anarchy.

Wheatley (111)

⤷⤶

People learn most rapidly when they have a genuine sense of responsibility for their actions.

Senge (101)

⤷⤶

Deliberation should be joint; decision single.

Peter Drucker

⤷⤶

Empowerment is all about *letting go* so that others can *get going*.

Jack Welsh

⤷⤶

While management often delegates authority to make more time to concentrate on the development tasks that are their primary concern, management should never forget that they can only delegate authority and not responsibility.

Mizuno (80)

⤷⤶

QC is everybody's job.

Feigenbaum (29)

⤷⤶

Organizations of the future must rely more and more upon commitment to the participative problem solving process rather than submission to "command authority."

Lippitt (74)

⤷⤶

Authority is built upon subordination. People must be willing to accept subordinate roles, limited definitions of themselves. And Americans everywhere are becoming insubordinate, unmanageable.

Cornuelle (14)

⤷⤶

Power is an essential ingredient in any organization or society; its absence results in chaos.

Wynn and Guditus (113)

⋏ᴏᴐᴧ

Neither the functional work groups nor the cross-function work groups should have the authority to superimpose decisions upon the other. Such use of authority leads to win-lose struggles, resentments, and maneuvering for power rather than to seeking solutions which will be in the best interests of the total corporation.

Likert (72)

⋏ᴏᴐᴧ

Power adheres to those who can cope with the critical problems of the organization. As such power is not a dirty secret, but the secret to success.

Jeffrey Pfeffer and Gerald Salancic

⋏ᴏᴐᴧ

When managers recognize that mere obedience to authority has become less acceptable to employees and that a sound approach to management that uses some other means of control is not only necessary but attainable, the solution to the productivity dilemma will be forthcoming. The solution is to reinvolve those who are responsible for decision making and productivity in the process of increasing productivity. To succeed, they must apply their thoughts, judgment, emotions, and skills to the task. They must participate.

Robert Blake and Jane Mouton

⋏ᴏᴐᴧ

Delegation is the process of building up people, then letting go of a responsibility. It sounds easy, but it almost never is. Egos get in the way.

McCormack (77)

⋏ᴏᴐᴧ

One might expect that any movement away from authoritarian control would be greatly appreciated by employees. Experience has shown, however, as have experiments, that when a management relinquishes tight controls and moves toward participative management, the *initial* response of members of the organization at every hierarchical level may be apathy or open hostility and aggressive responses against their superiors.

Likert (73)

⋏ᴏᴐᴧ

Quality Planning
(Quality by Design)

Good things only happen when planned; bad things happen on their own.
Crosby (16)

Good quality is never achieved by accident.
Ishihara (54)

An important feature of a good quality program is that it controls quality at the source.
Feigenbaum (29)

Plans are nothing. Planning is everything.
Dwight Eisenhower

If one does not know to which port one is sailing, no wind is favourable.
Seneca

There is no way to ensure quality or uniformity in the absence of a detailed design.

Lynn Shostack

∾∾

The price for ignoring the impact of design on service can be staggering.

Davidow and Uttal (17)

∾∾

Fanaticism consists in redoubling your effort when you have forgotten your aim.

George Santayana

∾∾

The thorns which I have reaped are of the tree I planted.

Lord Byron

∾∾

When we build, let us think that we build forever.

John Ruskin

∾∾

If you don't know where you are going, it doesn't much matter what you do.

Lewis Carroll

∾∾

Knowledge about what man has been and is can protect the future.

Margaret Mead

∾∾

Engineered like no other car in the world.

Mercedes Benz (slogan)

∾∾

Honda . . . we make it simple.

American Honda Motors (slogan)

∾∾

Inexpensive. And built to stay that way.

Subaru of America (slogan)

∾∾

Our goal is to build the highest quality cars and trucks in the world.

Ford Motor Co. (slogan)

∾∾

The power of intelligent engineering
(*Oldsmobile*) **General Motors** (slogan)

∾∾

Where quality is built in, not added on.
American Motors (slogan)

∾∾

You shouldn't call it a planning process, although what you get out of it is a plan. What you have accomplished is communication.
John Akers (IBM)

∾∾

Perfection of means and confusion of goals seem, in my opinion, to characterize our age.
Albert Einstein

∾∾

It's a bad plan that can't be changed.
Publilius Syrus

∾∾

Simplify, simplify.
Henry David Thoreau

∾∾

A danger foreseen is half avoided.
Thomas Fuller

∾∾

Everything should be made as simple as possible, but not simpler.
Albert Einstein

∾∾

An ounce of prevention is worth a pound of cure.
English Proverb

∾∾

Nothing can be done without a cause, nor has anything been done which cannot be done again. If that has been done which could be done, it ought not to be regarded as a prodigy. There are, therefore, no prodigies.
Cicero

∾∾

KISS: Keep It Simple, Stupid!
Anonymous

∾∾

I emphasize the importance of details. You must perfect every fundamental of your business if you expect it to perform well.
Ray Kroc (McDonald's)

ଚ∕ଚ

If you don't know where you are going, you might end up someplace else.
Lawrence Peter [Yogi] Berra

ଚ∕ଚ

Abstract planning divorced from action becomes a cerebral activity of conjuring up a world that does not exist.
Wheatley (111)

ଚ∕ଚ

People seldom hit what they do not aim at.
Henry David Thoreau

ଚ∕ଚ

Success is not an accident.
Robbins (95)

ଚ∕ଚ

The secret to preparing for success is no secret at all.
Robb E. Dalton

ଚ∕ଚ

Defining an objective is like telling a railroad ticket clerk your destination before you buy a ticket. If you have not decided on a destination, you cannot buy a ticket.
Ishihara (54)

ଚ∕ଚ

Planning is future-oriented, and the future will arrive whether the organization is ready or not.
Wynn and Guditus (113)

ଚ∕ଚ

If you don't know where you are going, any road'll get you there.
Anonymous

ଚ∕ଚ

Brevity is the sister of talent.
Anton Chekhov

ଚ∕ଚ

Teamwork/Employee Involvement

The intelligence of the team exceeds the intelligence of the individuals in the team.

Senge (101)

The really good team is more than the sum of its players. On an ordinary team, one plus one is two, but on the best team it is three. Rather than having one star, the whole team stars.

Osada

Teams outperform individuals acting alone or in larger organizational groupings, especially when performance requires multiple skills, judgments, and experiences.

Katzenbach and Smith (67)

The evidence strongly suggests that a consensus approach yields more creative decisions and more effective implementation than does individual decision making.

William Ouchi

Teams provide possibilities for empowerment that are not available to individual employees.

Wellins, Byham, and Wilson (110)

In a civilized society, we all depend upon each other.

Samuel Johnson

Teams are more powerful learning entities than individuals seeking to learn on their own.

Murgatroyd and Morgan (81)

Instead of a pyramid . . . the high value enterprise looks more like a spider's web.

Reich (93)

We trained hard, but it seemed that every time we were beginning to form up into teams we would be reorganized. I was to learn later in life that we tend to meet any new situation by reorganizing; and a wonderful method it can be for creating the illusion of progress while producing confusion, inefficiency and demoralization.

Caius Petronius

All for one, one for all.
(*Tout pour un, un pour tous.*)

Alexandre Dumas

Individual skills are combined so that the group's ability to innovate is something more than the simple sum of its parts.

Reich (93)

If I have seen further it is by standing on the shoulders of giants.

Isaac Newton

It is difference of opinion that makes horse races.

Mark Twain

When many are got together, you can be guided by him whose counsel is wisest. If a man is alone, he is less full of resource and his wit is weaker.

Homer

᪣

Few incentives are more powerful than membership in a small group engaged in a common task, sharing the risks of defeat and the potential rewards of victory.

Reich (93)

᪣

There are no hidden politics in the team.

Murgatroyd and Morgan (81)

᪣

It takes two to speak the truth—one to speak and another to hear.

Henry David Thoreau

᪣

The business relies less on procedures, forms, and technology and more upon the cohesiveness of its people.

Baker (4)

᪣

No team is an island within an organization.

Murgatroyd and Morgan (81)

᪣

No man is an island, entire of itself; every man is a piece of the continent, a part of the main.

John Donne

᪣

A striker who leads the attack places himself in the right position, receives a pass from one of his teammates, and in midair kicks the ball and scores. The fans go wild. Who scored that goal? Most people would say the striker scored that goal. A good coach would say the team scored that goal.

Aguayo (1)

᪣

If you want a thing done well, do it yourself.

Napoleon Bonaparte

᪣

United we stand, divided we fall.

Aesop

People never know each other until they have eaten a certain amount of salt together.

Aristotle

There are many objects of great value to man which cannot be attained by unconnected individuals, but must be attained, if attained at all, by association.

Daniel Webster

Union gives strength.

Aesop

Behind an able man there are always other able men.

Chinese Proverb

Too many cooks spoil the broth.

English Proverb

Hand rubs hand and hand washes hand.
(*Manus manum fricat, et manus manum lavat.*)

Latin Proverb

Three helping one another bear the burden of six.

George Herbert

When was ever honey made with one bee in a hive?

Thomas Hood

Two dogs will kill a lion.

Hebrew Proverb

Many hands make light work.

English Proverb

Many hands make the burden light.
(*Multae manus onus levius faciunt.*)
Latin Proverb

ⱥⱥⱥ

The best partner for dice-playing is not a just man, but a good dice-player.
Plato

ⱥⱥⱥ

It is good to rub and polish your mind against the minds of others.
Montaigne

ⱥⱥⱥ

In the last analysis, [the HP way] is a feeling that everyone is part of a team, and that team is HP.
Hewlett and Packard (47)

ⱥⱥⱥ

People can be themselves only in small, comprehensible groups.
Schumacher (99)

ⱥⱥⱥ

Two heads are better than one.
English Proverb

ⱥⱥⱥ

No one can know everything.
Horace

ⱥⱥⱥ

The pope and a peasant know more between them than the pope alone.
Italian Proverb

ⱥⱥⱥ

None of us exists independent of our relationships with others.
Wheatley (111)

ⱥⱥⱥ

A committee faced with a major decision can't always move as quickly as the events it's trying to respond to. By the time the committee is ready to shoot, the duck has flown away.
Iacocca (52)

ⱥⱥⱥ

The face-to-face group is as significant a unit of organization as the individual. The two are not antithetical. In a genuinely effective group the individual finds some of his deepest satisfaction.

McGregor (79)

∽ை஦ை

Much of what we speak of as individual achievement takes place in a team context.

Gardner (32)

∽ை஦ை

Teamwork throughout any organization is an essential component of the implementation of TQM for it builds up trust, improves communication and develops independence.

John Oakland

∽ை஦ை

Teams become the engines of quality improvement.

Sallis (96)

∽ை஦ை

Just putting a bunch of people in a room together does not a team make!

Gitlow and Gitlow (36)

∽ை஦ை

Teams are the real guts of TQM because they work to fix the fundamental flaws that prevent customer delight.

Berry (6)

∽ை஦ை

The problem of the group versus the individual is not an either-or problem at all. There are kinds of activities which are appropriate to the individual, others that are appropriate to the pair, and others that are appropriate to larger groups.

McGregor (79)

∽ை஦ை

Teams do not become teams just because we call them teams or send them to team-building workshops.

Katzenbach and Smith (67)

∽ை஦ை

Business is very much a team sport. Some people are managers, some are players, and some are support—but they all have to do their jobs if the team expects to win.

Osada (85)

⋄୧ୡ⋄

Science is rooted in conversations. The cooperation of different people may culminate in scientific results of the utmost importance.

Werner Heisenberg

⋄୧ୡ⋄

Those who see teams as a replacement for hierarchy are missing the true potential of teams.

Katzenbach and Smith (67)

⋄୧ୡ⋄

I see us moving toward a team-oriented, multiskilled environment in which the team takes on many of the supervisor's and trainer's tasks. If you combine that with some sort of gain sharing, you probably will have a much more productive plant with higher employee satisfaction and commitment.

Robert Hass (Levi Strauss)

⋄୧ୡ⋄

Much of the wisdom of teams lies in the disciplined pursuit of performance.

Katzenbach and Smith (67)

⋄୧ୡ⋄

The process of arriving at consensus is a free and open exchange of ideas which continues until agreement has been reached. This process assumes that each individual's concerns are heard and understood and that a sincere attempt has been made to take them into consideration in the search for and the formulation of a conclusion. This conclusion may not reflect the exact wishes of each member, but since it does not violate the deep concerns of anyone, it can be agreed upon by all.

Rensis Likert and Jane Likert

⋄୧ୡ⋄

Performance . . . is the primary objective while a team remains the means, not the end.

Katzenbach and Smith (67)

⋄୧ୡ⋄

If you have a horse and a wagon you have three things: a horse, a wagon, and a horse-wagon.
Chinese Proverb

Good personal chemistry or the desire to "become a team," for example, can foster teamwork values, but teamwork is not the same thing as a team.
Katzenbach and Smith (67)

Voting has no place in the consensus-building process. Voting is a convenient way of disposing of an issue with dispatch, but it commonly suppresses conflict rather than resolves it.
Wynn and Guditus (113)

Teams are not antithetical to individual performance. Real teams always find ways for each individual to contribute and thereby gain distinction.
Katzenbach and Smith (67)

Work teams don't spring up overnight.
Wellins, Byham, and Wilson (110)

Teams and performance are an unbeatable combination.
Katzenbach and Smith (67)

In essence, a team that is just starting out is not really a team, even though everyone might call it one. . . . Don't fool yourself.
Wellins, Byham, and Wilson (110)

Teams should be formed only when an achievable goal with a specific objective can be identified.
Harrington-Mackin (45)

Groups do not become teams simply because someone labels them as teams.
Katzenbach and Smith (67)

True teamwork occurs in situations where members are performance-dependent on each other. It is not simply a togetherness.

Buchholz and Roth (8)

෩

Teams offer greater participation, challenge, and feelings of accomplishment. Organizations with teams will attract and retain the best people. The others will have to do without.

Wellins, Byham, and Wilson (110)

෩

Decision making by consensus should be the basic policy.

Likert (72)

෩

To create a high-performance team, it is important that the work to be performed does rely on teamwork rather than on isolated, individual efforts.

Buchholz and Roth (8)

෩

No matter what your business, those teams are the wave of the future.

Jerry Junkins (Texas Instruments)

෩

Groups become teams through *disciplined action.*

Katzenbach and Smith (67)

෩

If you really believe in quality, when you cut through everything, it's empowering your people, and it's empowering your people that leads to teams.

Jamie Houghton (Corning)

෩

Perhaps the biggest reason for the movement toward empowered work teams is the fact that teams work.

Wellins, Byham, and Wilson (110)

෩

[A multiple overlapping group structure] requires group decision making by consensus in all work groups throughout the organization.

Likert (72)

෩

Employee involvement is moving from the stage of curious
experimentation to one of business necessity.
                    Wellins, Byham, and Wilson (110)

Leadership by consensus is not for everybody.
                    Wynn and Guditus (113)

[People] are never so likely to settle a question rightly as when they
discuss it freely.
                    Lord Thomas Macaulay

Coordination and productive use of differences should be achieved by
group decision making processes used skillfully throughout the company.
                    Likert (72)

The absence of broader involvement can, and frequently does, jeopardize
successful implementation of even a highly appropriate solution.
                    Wynn and Guditus (113)

Most so-called managerial teams are not teams at all, but collections of
individual relationships with the boss in which each individual is vying
with every other for power, prestige, recognition, and personal autonomy.
                    McGregor (79)

The leader makes the team.
                    Mary Parker Follett

Consensus management shifts the emphasis away from leadership as a
position and toward leadership as a function.
                    Wynn and Guditus (113)

The greater the loyalty of the members of a group toward the group, the
greater is the motivation among the members to achieve the goals of the
group, and the greater the probability that the group will achieve its goals.
                    Likert (72)

The team concept conveys the message that PQI [= Productivity and Quality Improvement] is everybody's business.
Hradesky (49)

꽃

Competition leads to loss. People pulling in opposite directions on a rope only exhaust themselves: they go nowhere.
Deming (21)

꽃

A camel is a horse designed by a committee.
Anonymous

꽃

It is not possible simply to order subordinates to behave like a team.
Pascale and Athos (86)

꽃

Major gains in quality and productivity most often result from teams.
Scholtes (98)

꽃

No grand idea was ever born in a conference, but a lot of foolish ideas have died there.
F. Scott Fitzgerald

꽃

Committee—a group of men who individually can do nothing but as a group decide that nothing can be done.
Fred Allen

꽃

As a spirit of teamwork invades the organization, employees everywhere will begin working together toward quality—no barriers, no factions, "all one team" moving together in the same direction.
Scholtes (98)

꽃

Through teamwork and group activity many of the difficult organizational problems of coordination and control can be solved.
McGregor (79)

꽃

A committee is a group of the unwilling, chosen from the unfit, to do the unnecessary.

Anonymous

∽᎐᎐∽

People:
The Individual
Worker

In the high-value enterprise, only one asset grows more valuable as it is used: the problem-solving, -identifying, and brokering skills of key people.
Reich (93)

My first message is: Listen, listen, listen to the people who do the work.
H. Ross Perot

I believe the real differences between success and failure in a corporation can very often be traced to the question of how well the organization brings out the great energies and talents of its people.
Thomas Watson Jr. (IBM)

Only through the collective efforts of their individual members do companies change; companies are incapable of changing themselves.

Hunt (50)

⮞⟡⮜

To find out how to improve productivity, quality and performance—ask the people who do the work.

Harvard Business Review

⮞⟡⮜

Quality is made by the hands of operators.

Ishihara (54)

⮞⟡⮜

Despite what the textbooks say, most important decisions in corporate life are made by individuals, not by committees.

Iacocca (52)

⮞⟡⮜

Marvels are many, but man is the greatest.

Sophocles

⮞⟡⮜

Believe one who knows by experience.
(*Experto credite.*)

Virgil

⮞⟡⮜

The difference between people who exercise initiative and those who don't is literally the difference between night and day.

Covey (15)

⮞⟡⮜

A man cannot make a pair of shoes rightly unless he do it in a devout manner.

Thomas Carlyle

⮞⟡⮜

One good head is better than a hundred strong hands.

Thomas Fuller

⮞⟡⮜

Those who *implement* the plans must make the plans.

Patrick Haggerty (Texas Instruments)

⮞⟡⮜

We assume people are adults.

James Treybig (Tandem)

❧

Respect for the dignity of our people demands that we answer some simple and universal questions:

What do you expect of me?
What's in it for me?
Where do I go with a problem?

Fred Smith (Federal Express)

❧

Any change the workers make to the plan is fatal to success.

Frederick Taylor

❧

Innovation and creativity are the lifeblood of a firm's existence and the source of future profits. They germinate only in the fertile soil of the human mind.

Ernst & Young (27)

❧

Most managers are reluctant to let their people run with the ball. But you'd be surprised how fast an informed and motivated guy can run.

Iacocca (52)

❧

Absolute prediction and uniformity are, therefore, impossible. While this may feel slightly unsettling, it certainly makes for a more interesting world. People go from being predictable to being surprising.

Wheatley (111)

❧

Thinking is the hardest work there is, which is the probable reason so few engage in it.

Henry Ford (Ford)

❧

There is no expedient to which a man will not go to avoid the real labor of thinking.

Thomas Edison

❧

Man will exercise self-direction and self-control in the service of objectives to which he is committed.

McGregor (Theory Y)

ꙮ

If we all did the things we are capable of doing, we would literally astound ourselves.

Thomas Edison

ꙮ

High-quality companies treat their human resource as a resource, not a commodity.

George (35)

ꙮ

Any supervisor worth his salt would rather deal with people who attempt too much than with those who try too little.

Iacocca (52)

ꙮ

The most difficult problem to solve is employee indifference: people closing their eyes and choosing to do nothing.

Ishihara (54)

ꙮ

Common sense is genius in its working clothes.

Thomas Edison

ꙮ

Group participation is satisfying and rewarding, but let's not forget what has made the world move forward—the individual.

Harrington (44)

ꙮ

The skills of the work force are going to be the key competitive weapon in the twenty-first century.

Thurow (103)

ꙮ

The old smokestack division of a firm into "heads" and "hands" no longer works. The knowledge load and, more important, the decision load, are being redistributed. In a continual circle of learning and unlearning, workers need to master new technologies, adapt to new organizational forms, and generate new ideas.

Toffler (104)

ᰍᰍ

A company is no better or no worse than the employees it has.

Ishikawa (56)

ᰍᰍ

Skilled people become the only sustainable competitive advantage.

Thurow (103)

ᰍᰍ

If management thinks people don't care, it's likely that people won't care.

F. James McDonald (General Motors Corporation)

ᰍᰍ

Almost every great breakthrough has been the result of an individual's efforts, not group activities. When management loses sight of individuals, they lose sight of reality.

Harrington (44)

ᰍᰍ

An expert is someone who knows some of the worst mistakes that can be made in his subject and who manages to avoid them.

Werner Heisenberg

ᰍᰍ

Quality Improvement (Innovation)

Creativity is thinking up new things. Innovation is doing new things.
Levitt (71)

Improvement means the organized creation of beneficial change; the attainment of unprecedented levels of performance. A synonym is *breakthrough*.
Juran (64)

Quality improvement at a revolutionary pace is now becoming simply good management.
Godfrey (38)

Even if you're on the right track, you'll get run over if you just sit there.
Will Rogers

When we stop improving, we start to slip backward.
Harrington (44)

⟡

A corporation cannot be "excellent" in the sense of having arrived at a permanent excellence; it is always in the state of practicing the disciplines of learning, of becoming better or worse.
Senge (101)

⟡

If you do what you've always done, you'll get what you've always gotten.
Anonymous

⟡

Technology is the answer—now what is the question?
R. Paul

⟡

Technology of itself is not necessarily a strategy for improvement—it is what technology is intended to do that counts.
Murgatroyd and Morgan (81)

⟡

He that will not apply new remedies, must expect new evils; for time is the greatest innovator.
Francis Bacon

⟡

Moderation is a fatal thing . . . Nothing succeeds like excess.
Oscar Wilde

⟡

What is now proved was once only imagined.
William Blake

⟡

Innovate is not to reform.
Edmund Burke

⟡

All good things which exist are the fruits of originality.
John Stuart Mill

⟡

The great truths begin as blasphemies.
Bernard Shaw

❧

The hope and not the fact of advancement is the spur of industry.
Robert Southey

❧

Management's job is not to promote satisfaction with the way things are but to create dissatisfaction with the way things are and could be.
Baker (4)

❧

Ford has a better idea.
Ford Motor Co. (slogan)

❧

The relentless pursuit of perfection.
(*Lexus*) *Toyota Motor Sales* (slogan)

❧

This isn't your father's Oldsmobile.
(*Oldsmobile*) *General Motors* (slogan)

❧

We just couldn't leave well enough alone.
Toyota Motor Sales (slogan)

❧

Continuous improvement is nothing but the development of ever better methods.
Walton (106)

❧

You get the good things first from Chrysler Corp.
Chrysler Corp. (slogan)

❧

Innovation working for you.
3M Corp. (slogan)

❧

Progress is our most important product.
General Electric (slogan)

❧

Where ideas unlock the future.
                    Bendix Corp. (slogan)
                         ∾ℭℰ∾

Just slightly ahead of our time.
                (*Panasonic*) **Matsushita** (slogan)
                         ∾ℭℰ∾

Casio. Where the miracles never cease.
                (*Casio watches*) **Casio Inc.** (slogan)
                         ∾ℭℰ∾

Continuous improvement is simply the way the company does business.
                         Walton (106)
                         ∾ℭℰ∾

To profesy is extremely difficult—especially with respect to the future.
                      Chinese Proverb
                         ∾ℭℰ∾

Develop a healthy disrespect for the impossible.
                   Gene Hoffman (Super Valu)
                         ∾ℭℰ∾

The big opportunities that lead to renewal, and the strategic decisions
that capture them, seem more like the whimsical flight of a butterfly
than the path of a carefully aimed arrow.
                       Waterman (107)
                         ∾ℭℰ∾

If a man write a better book, preach a better sermon, or make a better
mousetrap than his neighbor, tho' he builds his house in the woods, the
world will make a beaten path to his door.
                    Ralph Waldo Emerson
                         ∾ℭℰ∾

It is always the last song that an audience applauds the most.
                          Homer
                         ∾ℭℰ∾

The true creator is necessity, which is the mother of our invention.
                          Plato
                         ∾ℭℰ∾

What's past is prologue.
William Shakespeare
∾

It's a long road that has no turning.
English Proverb
∾

No great discovery was ever made without a bold guess.
Isaac Newton
∾

Hats off to the past; coats off to the future.
American Proverb
∾

Invention breeds invention.
Ralph Waldo Emerson
∾

Learn to unlearn.
Benjamin Disraeli
∾

The mind is slow to unlearn what it has been long in learning.
Seneca
∾

Necessity is the mother of invention.
Jonathan Swift
∾

Men, my brothers, men the workers
ever reaping something new:
That which they have done
but earnest of the things that they shall do.
Alfred Lord Tennyson
∾

And in such indexes, although small pricks
To their subsequent volumes, there is seen
The baby figure of the giant mass
Of things to come at large.
William Shakespeare
∾

You have to believe in the impossible.
> ***Howard Head*** (Head sports equipment)

❧❧❧

The new idea either finds a champion or dies.
> ***Edward Schon***

❧❧❧

There is no doubt that there is no right improvement tool for all operations and/or situations. The company that hangs its reputation on one is doomed to eventual extinction.
> ***Ernst & Young*** (27)

❧❧❧

Quality improvement is a fragile process. All major processes are.
> ***Sallis*** (96)

❧❧❧

Some men see things as they are, and say, "Why?" I dream of things that never were, and say, "Why not?"
> ***Bernard Shaw***

❧❧❧

In setting a target, usually the higher it is, the better it is.
> ***Nemoto*** (83)

❧❧❧

Nothing happens unless first a dream.
> ***Carl Sandburg***

❧❧❧

Improvement is made over what has already been improved. It is a continuous process and we never let up on it the entire year. Improvement means nothing more and nothing less.
> ***Nemoto*** (83)

❧❧❧

A mighty flame followeth a tiny spark.
> ***Dante***

❧❧❧

The ancestor of every action is a thought.
> ***Ralph Waldo Emerson***

❧❧❧

I am firmly convinced that the seeds for improvement are limitless.

Nemoto (83)

⌁

Make sure you have a Vice President in Charge of Revolution, to engender ferment among your more conventional colleagues.

Ogilvy (84)

⌁

Imagination is more important than knowledge. For knowledge is limited, whereas imagination embraces the entire world.

Albert Einstein

⌁

Shallow men believe in luck, believe in circumstances. Strong men believe in cause and effect.

Ralph Waldo Emerson

⌁

An idea that has been brought to this [implementation] stage but not implemented is like a picture of a delicious cake.

Ishihara (54)

⌁

Basically, there are two ways to make improvements. One is what might be called the silver bullet method. This is a massive overhaul that roots out all the problems and puts everything right in one fell swoop.

. . . When you are not feeling well, you may have to take medicine to get back on track. But it is even more important that you have good habits to stay fit. Get lots of sleep. Exercise. Eat the right foods. The proper habits, like the ancient Chinese herbal remedies, are long-term cures to keep you in good health. And this is the second type of improvement.

Osada (85)

⌁

The best way to predict the future is to create it.

Peter Drucker

⌁

Anyone who can spell a word only one way is an idiot.

W. C. Fields

⌁

To achieve improvement at a revolutionary pace requires that improvement be made mandatory—that is become a part of the regular job, written into the job description.
Juran (65)

∾ை∾

What's new for tomorrow is at Singer today.
Singer Co. (slogan)

∾ை∾

One of the basic principles of kaizen . . . is the phrase "do it," or in Japanese, "ya re." What this means is that the problem-solving or continuous process need not take a long time. Some people and organizations get hung up on taking every decision down to the very finest degree. The result is frequently that nothing gets done: paralysis by analysis.
Forsha (31)

∾ை∾

Chaos often breeds life, when order breeds habit.
Henry Brooks Adams

∾ை∾

Quality Control

Quality needs to be constantly improved, but it is just as necessary to make sure that quality never deteriorates.

Mizuno (80)

Self checking is always vital. A central tenet of TQM is that the person doing the work is responsible for the results obtained. Responsibility cannot be said to have been exercised if the individual hands over his/her work in an unknown or uncorrected state.

Allan Sayle

The word "maintenance" has a nuance suggesting maintenance of status quo and doing nothing at all to change things. But that is an erroneous assumption. If you do nothing, you cannot even maintain the status quo.

Nemoto (83)

Quality control and standardization are extremely closely linked.

Hosotani (48)

Variation in a process (or product/service) is natural; it should be expected. But, it is a wild beast that must be controlled.

Gitlow and Gitlow (36)

❧

Different people in the same structure tend to produce qualitatively similar products.

Senge (101)

❧

Self-generated quality control is more effective than inspector-generated quality control.

Peters (87)

❧

Be thorough; take nothing for granted. Be suspicious of experience and "sixth sense;" be doubtful of tradition and intuition. "Question everything: product standards, raw materials standards, tolerances, measurement instruments—*everything.*" That is the often-repeated motto of quality control.

Ishihara (54)

❧

Control and improvement are two wheels of the same cart.

Ishikawa (55)

❧

One axiom has been apparent from the beginning of man's effort to make things. That axiom is: NO TWO THINGS ARE ALIKE; THEY WILL ALWAYS VARY. Anyone who has ever tried to work with supposedly identical items will eventually come to this discovery, and that is why manufacturers generally appreciate this axiom.

Wheeler and Chambers (112)

❧

Brevity is the soul of wit.

William Shakespeare

❧

One thorn of experience is worth a whole wilderness of warning.

James Russell Lowell

❧

Men acquire a particular quality by constantly acting in a particular way.

Aristotle

❦

The palest ink is clearer than the best memory.

Chinese Proverb

❦

Control consists in verifying whether everything occurs in conformity with the plan adopted, the instructions issued and the principles established.

Henri Fayol

❦

The rung of a ladder was never meant to rest upon, but only to hold a man's foot long enough to enable him to put the other somewhat higher.

Thomas Huxley

❦

Everyone is in a state of self-control to a greater or lesser extent. Thanks to this ability of self-control, we humans can enjoy our lives, including sports and leisure. Of course, education and training are to a certain extent necessary to cultivate the self-control capacity of the workers.

Kondo (68)

❦

The proactive approach to a mistake is to acknowledge it instantly, correct and learn from it.

Covey (15)

❦

Sometimes when I consider what tremendous consequences come from little things . . . I am tempted to think . . . there are no little things.

Bruce Barton

❦

That which we persist in doing becomes easier—not that the nature of the task has changed, but our ability to do has increased.

Ralph Waldo Emerson

❦

Things are always at their best in the beginning.

Blaise Pascal

❦

What is done well is done quickly enough.
Augustus Caesar

All that is human must retrograde if it does not advance.
Edward Gibbon

The road to ruin is always kept in good repair.
Anonymous

Nothing under the sun is ever accidental.
G. E. Lessing

Nothing so bad but it might be worse.
English Proverb

Nothing maintains its bloom forever; age succeeds to age.
Cicero

Poverty comes from God, but not dirt.
Hebrew Proverb

Be sure you are right, then go ahead.
David Crockett

An environment which calls for perfection is not likely to be easy. But aiming for it is always a goad to progress.
Thomas Watson Jr. (IBM)

Everything we do that relates to quality is central to quality control, yet our efforts should be directed to prevention rather than correction.
Mizuno (80)

Do not let the tiniest problem escape your notice. Remember: little brooks grow into mighty rivers.
Ishihara (54)

Incessantly reacting to problems after the fact is like seeing the fire without seeing the tinder or seeing the first spark. The fire is a problem, of course, but it would not have happened if the spark and the tinder had not been neglected for so long.

Osada (85)

Quality control is the art of doing the obvious and doing it right.

Mizuno (80)

If the target is not correct, control of results is impossible.

Nakamura (82)

Control is correcting the cause, not treating the effect.

Mizuno (80)

For quality in the sense of freedom from deficiencies, the long-range goal is perfection.

Juran (61)

"You've got to ac-cent-tchu-ate the positive
Elim-my-nate the negative."

Johnny Mercer

To survive in today's competitive era of rapidly changing product models (some factories seldom make the same products two months in a row), factories must adopt wide-variety, small-lot production. This kind of production only runs smoothly with an accelerated cycle of discovering problems, finding causes, implementing countermeasures, and revising standards.

Nakamura (82)

Control without action is simply a hobby.

Ishikawa (57)

Process-Oriented Management Versus Results-Oriented Management

Many of our business leaders still come from the days of the fifties and sixties when meeting production and schedules were the only major concerns. Consumers in those days just bought—bought—bought. Producers just produced—produced—produced. When it broke we bought another one.

Stratton (102)

Do not worry about the results, but be concerned with the process.

Nemoto (83)

He who runs his company on visible figures alone will soon have neither company nor visible figures to work with.

W. Edwards Deming

The problem is not the result but the process.
Hosotani (48)

Products have limited lifespans, and even the best soon become obsolete. It is not products but the processes that create products that bring companies long-term success.
Hammer and Champy (43)

Golfers who ignore the mechanics of their swing and note only how far the ball has traveled are routinely confounded by their inability to predict or control the outcome of their efforts. The same can be said of business leaders who care only about results.
Chang, Labovitz, and Rosansky (13)

If the process is right, the results will take care of themselves.
Osada (85)

Running a company by profit alone is like driving a car by looking in the rearview mirror. It tells you where you've been, not where you are going.
Aguayo (1)

Quality comes not from inspection but from improvement of the process.
Walton (106)

Total conformance to specifications comes only by aiming at continuous process improvement.
Wheeler and Chambers (112)

Management that tries to induce people to meet the specifications is reacting to the situation knee-jerk fashion.
Aguayo (1)

Managers don't love the product.
Frederick Herzberg

Some say, "You only get what you measure." I say, "And that's all you get!"

Stratton (102)

⌑

You may recall that Vasili Alexeyev was a Russian superheavyweight weight lifter. He was given a reward for each world record that he broke. He knew exactly what to do—he broke a lot of world records. But he broke them a gram or two at a time.

Scherkenbach (97)

⌑

I always ask this question of the measurement advocates: "If you're so enamored with measuring people why don't you tell them you'll let them go home when they meet their bogie?" Most people would be home by 2:00 P.M. in a normal workday.

Stratton (102)

⌑

Leadership by consensus views process as being as important as product. That is, the impact of the process by which decisions are made will have a far-reaching effect on the quality of the product.

Wynn and Guditus (113)

⌑

Invention is only the beginning. Product reengineering and cloning are driving the product technology advantage out and the process technology advantage in.

Godfrey (38)

⌑

You can't drive a good work force 30 percent harder, but we've found that we could often work 30 or 50 or even 150 percent smarter.

Walter A. Fallon (Eastman Kodak)

⌑

Inspection, quotas, pep talks or threats are now all useless.

Aguayo (1)

⌑

Call a thing immoral or ugly, soul-destroying or a degradation of man, a peril to the peace of the world or to the well-being of future generations: as long as you have not shown it to be "uneconomic" you have not really questioned its right to exist, grow, and prosper.

Schumacher (99)

⌑

Quality improvement will result from people improving their processes
and from management improving the system.

Pyzdek (92)

Moments
of Truth

The moment of Truth: Any episode in which the customer comes into contact with some aspect of the organization and gets an impression of its service.

Karl Albrecht

SAS is you [the frontline people]. In the mind of the customer, you are the company at that particular moment of truth. I want you to respond to the real need of the customer, and not use some standardized procedure for getting rid of him.

Jan Carlzon

When an employee's eyes glaze over and he refuses a customer's request because of "company policy," the social process—the moment of truth—screeches to a halt.

Davidow and Uttal (17)

There is no longer any such thing as the customer; there is only this customer, the one with whom a seller is dealing at the moment and who now has the capacity to indulge his or her own personal tastes.
Hammer and Champy (43)

୨୧

SAS has ten million passengers a year. The average passenger comes in contact with five SAS employees. Therefore, SAS is the product of the ten million times the five. SAS is fifty million "moments of truth" per year.
Jan Carlzon (SAS)

୨୧

He gives twice who gives soon.
Publilius Syrus

୨୧

Europe's most helpful airline.
Sabena (slogan)

୨୧

SAS is the contact of one person in the market and one person at SAS. That is SAS.
Jan Carlzon (SAS)

୨୧

Service. The ultimate luxury.
Marriott (slogan)

୨୧

When the moments of truth go unmanaged, the quality of service regresses to mediocrity.
Albrecht and Zemke (2)

୨୧

IThe true test of an organization's commitment to service quality isn't the stylishness of the pledge it makes in its marketing literature; it's the way the company responds when things go wrong for the customer.
Ron Zemke

୨୧

We have 50,000 moments of truth out there every day.
Jan Carlzon (SAS)

୨୧

The concept of managing the moments of truth is the very essence of service management.

Albrecht and Zemke (2)

სოელ

The dependability people.

Maytag Co. (slogan)

სოელ

Customer service gets great lip service.

Davidow and Uttal (17)

სოელ

Your anywhere, anything, anytime network.

AT&T (slogan)

სოელ

Make yourself necessary to someone.

Ralph Waldo Emerson

სოელ

The end result of a service is a feeling.

Karl Albrecht

სოელ

The moment of truth in the customer's view of the world is a sense of discrepancy between what is expected or desired and what is occurring.

Murgatroyd and Morgan (81)

სოელ

Change:
Need/Resistance

Change is what makes the world go round, not love—love only keeps it populated.

Charles Brower

If change is to occur, it must come about through hard work within the organization itself.

Lippitt (74)

In the process of change, as in any other process, each step must be taken in turn. To attempt step two before completing step one is like trying to wax your car before you have washed it. The result will not be pretty. To apply this process to the wrong issue is like waxing your pet cockatiel.

Forsha (31)

If you think you are going to be successful running your business in the next 10 years the way you [did] in the last 10 years, you're out of your mind. To succeed, we have to disturb the present.
                          Roberto Goizueta (Coca-Cola)

Vision without action is merely a dream. Action without vision just passes the time. Vision with action can change the world!
                          Joel Barker

It is impossible to step twice into the same river.
                          Heraclitus

A fixation on what was can blind us to what is, blocking the recognition of change.
                          Reich (93)

Organizations are dynamically conservative: that is to say, they fight like mad to remain the same. Only when an organization cannot repel, ignore, contain or transform the threat, it responds to it. But the characteristic is that of least change: nominal or token change.
                          Donald Schon

Reformers have the idea that change can be achieved by brutal sanity.
                          Bernard Shaw

All things flow; nothing abides.
                          Heraclitus

Change is not made without inconvenience, even from worse to better.
                          Richard Hooker

One fifth of the people are against everything all the time.
                          Robert Kennedy

Life can only be understood backwards; but it must be lived forwards.
                          Sören Kierkegaard

The reasonable man adapts himself to the world; the unreasonable one persists in trying to adapt the world to himself. Therefore all progress depends on the unreasonable man.

Bernard Shaw

Things do not change; we change.

Henry David Thoreau

There is nothing in this world constant, but inconstancy.

Jonathan Swift

There is nothing permanent except change.

Heraclitus

To change is to risk something. That makes us insecure. Not to change is the bigger risk, but it seldom feels that way.

Waterman (107)

Change is inevitable in a progressive society. Change is constant.

Disraeli

The future struggles against being mastered.

Latin Proverb

The only stability possible is stability in motion.

Gardner (32)

I like the dreams of the future better than the history of the past.

Thomas Jefferson

You ain't heard nothin' yet, folks.

Al Johnson

In the carriages of the past you can't go anywhere.

Maxim Gorky

Such is the state of life that none are happy but by the anticipation of change. The change itself is nothing: when we have made it the next wish is to change again.

Samuel Johnson

๛

Never swap horses crossing a stream.

American Proverb

๛

The more it changes, the more it remains the same.
(*Plus ça change, plus c'est la même chose.*)

French Proverb

๛

Discontent is the first step in the progress of a man or nation.

Oscar Wilde

๛

No army can withstand the strength of an idea whose time has come.

Victor Hugo

๛

Restlessness is the hallmark of existence.

Arthur Schopenhauer

๛

"Future shock". . . the shattering stress and disorientation that we induce in individuals by subjecting them to too much change in too short a time.

Toffler (104)

๛

You've got to be willing to fail.

James Burke (Johnson & Johnson)

๛

Change has become both pervasive and persistent. It *is* normality.

Hammer and Champy (43)

๛

Any time you sincerely want to make a change, the first thing you must do is to raise your standards.

Robbins (94)

๛

The process of change (like charity) begins with the individual.
Forsha (31)

࿐

There is a sort of river of things passing into being and Time is a violent torrent; no sooner is a thing brought to sight than it is swept by and another takes its place, and this too will be swept away.
Marcus Aurelius

࿐

Culture shock is what happens when a traveller suddenly finds himself in a place where yes may mean no, where a "fixed price" is negotiable, where to be kept waiting in an outer office is no cause for insult, where laughter may signify anger.
Toffler (104)

࿐

Contemporary
Sources

1. Rafael Aguayo, *Dr. Deming: The American Who Taught the Japanese About Quality* (New York: Fireside, 1991).

2. Karl Albrecht and Ron Zemke, *Service America!: Doing Business in the New Economy* (New York: Warner Books, 1990).

3. Chris Argyris, *Management and Organizational Development* (New York: McGraw-Hill, 1971).

4. Edward M. Baker, "Managing Human Performance." In *Juran's Quality Control Handbook*, edited by J. M. Juran and Frank M. Gryna (New York: McGraw-Hill, 1988).

5. Warren Bennis and Burt Nanus, *Leaders: The Strategies for Taking Charge* (New York: Harper & Row, 1985).

6. Thomas Berry, *Managing the Total Quality Transformation* (New York: McGraw-Hill, 1990).

7. Jerome S. Bruner, *The Process of Education* (New York: Vintage Books, 1963).

8. Steve Buchholz and Thomas Roth, *Creating the High-Performance Team* (New York: John Wiley & Sons, 1987).

9. James MacGregor Burns, *Leadership* (New York: Harper & Row, 1978).

10. William C. Byham and Jeff Cox, *Zapp!: The Lightning of Empowerment* (New York: Ballantine Books, 1992).

11. Peter Capezio and Debra Morehouse, *Taking the Mystery Out of TQM: A Practical Guide to Total Quality Management* (Hawthorne, N.J.: Career Press, 1993).

12. Jan Carlzon, *Moments of Truth* (New York: Harper & Row, 1989).

13. Y.S. Chang, George Labovitz, and Victor Rosansky, *Making Quality Work: A Leadership Guide for the Results-Driven Manager* (New York: HarperCollins, 1993).

14. Richard Cornuelle, *De-Managing America* (New York: Random House, 1975).

15. Steven Covey, *The 7 Habits of Highly Effective People* (New York: Fireside, 1990).

16. Philip Crosby, *Quality Is Free: The Art of Making Quality Certain* (New York: Mentor, 1980.)

17. William Davidow and Bro Uttal, *Total Customer Service: The Ultimate Weapon* (New York: Harper Perennial, 1990).

18. Ronald G. Day, *Quality Function Deployment: Linking a Company with Its Customers* (Milwaukee: ASQC Quality Press, 1993).

19. W. Edwards Deming, *Out of the Crisis* (Cambridge, Mass.: MIT Center for Advanced Engineering Study, 1986).

20. Deming, *Quality, Productivity, and Competitive Position* (Cambridge, Mass.: MIT Center for Advanced Engineering Study, 1982).

21. Deming, *The New Economics* (Cambridge, Mass.: MIT Center for Advanced Engineering Study, 1993).

22. Peter Drucker, *The Age of Discontinuity: Guidelines to Our Changing Society* (New York: Harper & Row, 1969).

23. Drucker, *The Practice of Management* (New York: Harper & Row, 1954).

24. Drucker, *Management: Tasks, Responsibilities, Practices* (New York: Harper & Row, 1974).

25. Drucker, *Adventures of a Bystander* (New York: Harper & Row, 1979).

26. Drucker, *The Frontiers of Management: Where Tomorrow's Decisions Are Being Shaped Today* (New York: E. P. Dutton, 1986).

27. The Ernst & Young Quality Improvement Consulting Group *Total Quality: An Executive's Guide for the 1990s* (Homewood, Ill.: Business One Irwin, 1990).

28. Bertie Everard and Geoffrey Morris, *Effective School Management: Management in Education* (London: Paul Chapman Publishing, 1990).

29. Armand Feigenbaum, *Total Quality Control* (New York: McGraw-Hill, 1983).

30. Henry Ford and Samuel Crowther, *My Life and Work* (New York: Doubleday, 1922).

31. Harry Forsha, *The Pursuit of Quality Through Personal Change* (Milwaukee: ASQC Quality Press, 1992).

32. John W. Gardner, *Excellence* (New York: Norton, 1987).

33. Charles Garfield, *Peak Performers: The New Heroes of American Business* (New York: William Morrow & Co., 1986).

34. Harold Geneen, *Managing* (New York: Doubleday, 1985).

35. Steven George, *The Baldrige Quality System: The Do-It-Yourself Way to Transform Your Business* (New York: John Wiley & Sons, 1992).

36. Howard Gitlow and Shelly Gitlow, *The Deming Guide to Quality and Competitive Position* (Englewood Cliffs, N.J.: Prentice Hall, 1987).

37. William Glasser, *Quality School: Managing Students Without Coercion* (New York: Perennial Library, 1990).

38. A. Blanton Godfrey, *At the Cutting Edge of Quality: Ten Clear Trends for Quality Over the Next Decade* (Wilton, Conn.: Juran Institute, 1993).

39. Godfrey, "Rediscovering the Fundamentals to Reinvent the Future." In *IMPRO®* (Wilton, Conn.: Juran Institute, 1994).

40. Daniel E. Griffiths, *Administrative Theory* (New York: Appleton-Century-Crofts, 1959).

41. John Guaspari, *The Customer Connection: Quality for the Rest of Us* (New York: AMACOM, 1988).

42. Lawrence R. Guinta and Nancy Praizler, *The QFD Book: The Team Approach to Solving Problems and Satisfying Customers Through Quality Function Deployment* (New York: AMACOM, 1993).

43. Michael Hammer and James Champy, *Reengineering the Corporation: A Manifesto for Business Revolution* (New York: HarperCollins, 1994).

44. H. James Harrington, *The Improvement Process: How America's Leading Companies Improve Quality* (New York: Mc-Graw-Hill, 1987).

45. Deborah Harrington-Mackin, *The Team Building Tool Kit: Tips, Tactics, and Rules for Effective Workplace Teams* (New York: AMACOM, 1994).

46. Peter Hay, *The Book of Business Anecdotes* (New York: Wing Books, 1993).

47. William R. Hewlett and David Packard, *The HP Way* (Palo Alto, Calif.: Hewlett-Packard, 1980).

48. Katsuya Hosotani, *The QC Problem Solving Approach: Solving Workplace Problems the Japanese Way* (Tokyo: 3A Corporation, 1989).

49. John Hradesky, *Productivity & Quality Improvement: A Practical Guide to Implementing Statistical Process Control* (New York: McGraw-Hill, 1988.

50. V. Daniel Hunt, *Managing for Quality: Integrating Quality and Business Strategy* (Homewood, Ill.: Business One Irwin, 1993).

51. David Hutchins, *Achieve Total Quality* (Cambridge, Mass.: Director Books, 1992).

52. Lee Iacocca and William Novak, *Iacocca: An Autobiography* (New York: Bantam Books, 1984).

53. Masaaki Imai, *Kaizen: The Key to Japan's Competitive Success* (New York: McGraw-Hill, 1986).

54. Katsuyoshi Ishihara, *Implementing Quality on the Shop Floor: A Practical Guide* (White Plains, N.Y.: Quality Resources, 1992).

55. Kaoru Ishikawa, *Guide to Quality Control* (Tokyo: Asian Productivity Organization, 1992).

56. Ishikawa, *What Is Total Quality Control?: The Japanese Way* (Englewood Cliffs, N.J.: Prentice Hall, 1985).

57. Ishikawa, *Introduction to Quality Control* (Tokyo: 3A Corporation, 1993).

58. Juran Institute, *Quality Benchmarks for Executives: Executive Planning Guide* (Wilton, Conn.: Juran Institute, 1991).

59. Juran Institute, resource guide (Wilton, Conn.: Juran Institute, 1991).

60. Juran Institute, *Re-engineering Processes for Competitive Advantage: Business Process Quality Management®* (Wilton, Conn.: Juran Institute, 1994).

61. J. M. Juran, *Juran on Planning for Quality* (New York: Free Press, 1988).

62. Juran, *Juran on Quality by Design: The New Steps for Planning Quality into Goods and Services* (New York: Free Press, 1992).

63. Juran, *Managerial Breakthrough* (30th anniversary edition) (New York: McGraw-Hill, 1995).

64. Juran, *Juran on Leadership for Quality: An Executive Handbook* (New York: Free Press, 1989).

65. Juran, "Made in USA: A Break in the Clouds." In *The Quest for Excellence* (Washington, D.C.: Feb. 1990).

66. Juran, "The Upcoming Century of Quality." In *ASQC 48th Annual Quality Congress* (Milwaukee: ASQC, 1994).

67. John Katzenbach and Douglas Smith, *The Wisdom of Teams: Creating the High-Performance Organization* (New York: HarperBusiness, 1994).

68. Yoshio Kondo, "Quality in Japan." In *Juran's Quality Control Handbook*, edited by J. M. Juran and Frank M. Gryna (New York: McGraw-Hill, 1988).

69. Ray Kroc, *Grinding It Out: The Making of McDonald's* (New York: Berkley, 1977).

70. Hitoshi Kume, *Statistical Methods for Quality Improvement* (Tokyo: Association for Overseas Technical Scholarship, 1992).

71. Theodore Levitt, *The Marketing Imagination* (New York: Free Press, 1983).

72. Rensis Likert, *The Human Organization: Its Management and Value* (New York: McGraw-Hill, 1967).

73. Likert, *New Patterns of Management* (New York: McGraw-Hill, 1961).

74. Gordon Lippitt, *Organizational Renewal: Achieving Viability in a Changing World* (Englewood Cliffs, N.J.: Prentice Hall, 1969).

75. Abraham Maslow, *Motivation and Personality* (New York: Harper & Row, 1987).

76. Maslow, *The Farther Reaches of Human Nature* (New York: Viking Press, 1975).

77. Mark McCormack, *What They Don't Teach You at Harvard Business School* (New York: Bantam Books, 1985).

78. McCormack, *What They Still Don't Teach You at Harvard Business School* (New York: Bantam Books, 1989).

79. Douglas McGregor, *The Human Side of Enterprise* (25th anniversary printing) (New York: McGraw-Hill, 1985).

80. Shigeru Mizuno, *Company-Wide Total Quality Control* (Tokyo: Asian Productivity Organization, 1992).

81. Stephen Murgatroyd and Colin Morgan, *Total Quality Management and the School* (Buckingham: Open University Press, 1993).

82. Shigeru Nakamura, *The New Standardization: Keystone of Continuous Improvement in Manufacturing* (Portland, Ore.: Productivity Press, 1993).

83. Masao Nemoto, *Total Quality Control for Management: Strategies and Techniques from Toyota and Toyoda Gosei* (Englewood Cliffs, N.J.: Prentice Hall, Inc., 1987).

84. David Ogilvy, *Confessions of an Advertising Man* (New York: Atheneum, 1980).

85. Takashi Osada, *The 5S's: Five Keys to a Total Quality Environment* (Tokyo: Asian Productivity Organization, 1993).

86. Richard Tanner Pascale and Anthony G. Athos, *The Art of Japanese Management* (London: Penguin Books, 1986).

87. Thomas J. Peters, *Thriving on Chaos* (New York: Alfred A. Knopf, 1987).

88. Peters and Nancy Austin, *A Passion for Excellence: The Leadership Difference* (New York: Warner Books, 1986).

89. Peters and Robert H. Waterman Jr., *In Search of Excellence: Lessons from America's Best-Run Companies* (New York: Warner Books, 1982).

90. Robert Pirsig, *Zen and the Art of Motorcycle Maintenance: An Inquiry into Values* (New York, Morrow, 1974).

91. Paul Plsek and Arturo Onnias, *Quality Improvement Tools: Problem-Solving/Glossary* (Wilton, Conn.: Juran Institute, 1989).

92. Thomas Pyzdek, *Pyzdek's Guide to SPC: Applications and Special Topics* (Tucson. Ariz.: Quality Publishing, 1992).

93. Robert B. Reich, *The Work of Nations: Preparing Ourselves for 21st Century Capitalism* (New York: Vintage Books, 1992).

94. Anthony Robbins, *Awaken the Giant Within: How to Take Immediate Control of Your Mental, Emotional, Physical, and Financial Destiny!* (New York: Simon & Schuster, 1992).

95. Robbins, *Unlimited Power* (New York: Ballantine Books, 1986).

96. Edward Sallis, *Total Quality Management in Education* (London: Kogan Page, 1993).

97. William Scherkenbach, *The Deming Route to Quality and Productivity: Road Maps and Roadblocks* (Washington, D.C.: CEEPress Books, 1990).

98. Peter R. Scholtes, *The Team Handbook* (Madison, Wisc.: Joiner Associates Inc., 1988).

99. Ernst F. Schumacher, *Small Is Beautiful: Economics as If People Mattered* (New York: Harper & Row, 1973).

100. Philip Selznick, *Leadership in Administration: A Sociological Interpretation* (New York: Harper & Row, 1957).

101. Peter Senge, *The Fifth Discipline: The Art and Practice of the Learning Organization* (New York: Doubleday, 1980).

102. A. Donald Stratton, *An Approach to Quality Improvement That Works* (Milwaukee: ASQC Quality Press, 1991).

103. Lester Thurow, *Head to Head: The Coming Economic Battle Among Japan, Europe, and America* (New York: William Morrow & Co., 1992).

104. Alvin Toffler, *Future Shock* (New York: Random House, 1971).

105. Patrick L. Townsend and Joan E. Gebhardt, *Quality in Action: 93 Lessons in Leadership, Participation, and Measurement* (New York: John Wiley & Sons, 1992).

106. Mary Walton, *Deming Management at Work* (New York: Perigee Books, 1991).

107. Robert H. Waterman Jr., *The Renewal Factor: How the Best Get and Keep the Competitive Edge* (New York: Bantam Books, 1988).

108. Thomas J. Watson, Jr., *A Business and Its Beliefs: The Ideas That Helped Build IBM* (New York: McGraw-Hill, 1963).

109. Karl E. Weick, *The Social Psychology of Organization* (New York: Random House, 1979).

110. Richard S. Wellins, William C. Byham, and Jeanne M. Wilson, *Empowered Teams: Creating Self-Directed Work Groups That Improve Quality, Productivity, and Participation* (San Francisco: Jossey Bass, 1991).

111. Margaret J. Wheatley, *Leadership and the New Science: Learning About Organization from an Orderly Universe* (San Francisco: Berret Koehler, Publishers, 1992).

112. Donald Wheeler and David Chambers, *Understanding Statistical Process Control* (Knoxville, Tenn.: SPC Press, 1986).

113. Richard Wynn and Charles Guditus, *Team Management: Leadership by Consensus* (Columbus, Oh.: Charles E. Merrill Publishing, 1984).

Author Index

Topic Index

Slogans—*continued*
  Bendix Corp., 190
  Casio Inc., 190
  Chrysler Corp., 189
  Continental Airlines, 2
  Corning, 79
  Delta Air Lines, 6
  Eastern Airlines, 157
  Eastman Kodak, 79
  Federal Express, 78
Slogans—*continued*
  Ford Motor Co., 25, 78, 79, 129,
    166, 189
  General Electric, 189
  General Motors, 3, 7, 25, 27, 34,
    79, 148, 167, 189
  Gerber Products Co., 6, 7
  Hertz Corp., 7
  Iberia, 6
  IBM, 85, 128
  Japan Air Lines, 78
  J. C. Penney and Co., 25
  Kmart Corp., 30
  Korean Air Lines, 78
  Marriott, 2, 206
  Matsushita, 190
  Maytag Co., 207
  Mercedes Benz, 166
  National Car Rental Systems, 7
  New York Times, The, 19
  Procter & Gamble, 79
  Saab Cars USA, 26
  SAA-South African Airways, 78
  Sabena, 206
  Shell Oil Co., 9
  Singer Co., 194
  Studebaker-Packard, 133
  Subaru of America, 166
  Toyota Motor Sales, 29, 189
  TWA, 3
  USAir, 5
  Yellow Pages, 81
Slogans, inadequacies of, 67, 70, 71,
    72
Small-lot production, 199
Solutions. *See* Problem solving
Spanish proverbs
  on facts, 134

  on failure, 87
Specifications, 19, 20, 22, 35, 202
Standards, 47–49
  customer setting of, 1
  ISO 9000 series, 18
  management and, 114
  problem solving and, 95
  quality control and, 195
  TQM and, 35
Statistical process control (SPC), 73,
    76
Statistical thinking, 141–42
Statistics, 141–42
Strategic management, 75
Strategic planning, 153
Suckers, customers as, 10
Surprise, and motivation, 54
Survival, 107, 151–54. *See also*
    Failures
Systems, 138, 204
Systems deficiencies, 59–62, 63, 72
Systems thinking, 60, 73, 93, 107,
    114

Taylor Model, 34
Team building, 111
Teamwork, 169–80
  authority and, 164
  collective professionalism of, 34
  failures of, 111
  feasible problems for, 86
  goals of, 162
  in Japan, 162
  motivation for, 53, 55
  organizational purpose and, 11,
    14
  performance of, 55, 175, 176, 177
  synergism for, 111
  time devoted to, 74
  training and, 45
Technology, 21, 47, 188, 203. *See
    also* Computers
Testing
  in advertising, 136
  final product, 20
Test-marketing, 13
Theory Y, 184